Religion, Politics, and the Christian Right

Religion, Politics, and the Christian Right

Post–9/11 Powers and American Empire

Mark Lewis Taylor

Fortress Press

Minneapolis

Still and always, for Nadia and Laura

∽◡◡∽

Scripture quotations are from the New Revised Standard Version Bible,
copyright © 1989 by the Division of Christian Education of the National
Council of the Churches of Christ in the USA and used by permission.

Cover art: Cross image © Barry David Marcus / SuperStock.
Map image © Photodisc/Getty Images. Both used by permission.

Author photo: Steven Good
Cover and interior design: Zan Ceeley

Library of Congress Cataloging-in-Publication Data
Taylor, Mark L. (Mark Lewis), –
Religion, politics, and the Christian right :
post-9/11 powers and American empire / Mark Lewis Taylor.
p. cm.
Includes bibliographical references (p.   ) and index.
ISBN 0-8006-3783-6 (hardcover : alk. paper)
—ISBN 0-8006-3776-3 (pbk. : alk. paper)
1. Christianity and politics—United States. 2. Conservatism—Religious
aspects—Christianity. 3. Conservatism—United States. I. Title.
BR526.T39 2005
261.7'0973—dc22
2005020030

The paper used in this publication meets the minimum requirements of
American National Standard for Information Sciences—Permanence of
Paper for Printed Library Materials, ANSI Z329.48-1984.

Manufactured in the U.S.A.
09   08   07   06   05   1   2   3   4   5   6   7   8   9   10

CONTENTS

PREFACE

Many see religious faith today as having a chokehold on people seeking global peace and justice. Christian and Muslim militants, American and Islamist fundamentalists, seem to be trying to outdo one another in proclaiming God to be at work in their own political projects. Too often the results are conflict, war, or being perpetually poised for war.

The power of these militant faiths to do damage is drawn from their believers' alliances with structures of violence—whether the militant faithful are those operating through the deadly networks of al-Qaeda or those who fuse a Christian nationalism with the lethal systems of violence purveyed by U.S. military forces. The differences between al-Qaeda and U.S. military forces are numerous, of course, but the ways significant leaders from both groups fuse their religion with political visions are often strikingly similar. It can seem, indeed, that we face not so much the "clash of civilizations" that Samuel P. Huntingdon made famous, but more the "clash of fundamentalisms" that Tariq Ali has explored.[1]

This book concerns especially the U.S. variant of militant faith, often called "the Christian Right," as it has embraced ever more strident political and moral tones in early twenty-first-century U.S. government. As I shall document, this is a government that today announces a near perpetual "war on terror," rationalizes interrogation procedures that amount to torture, and generally pursues a unilateralist foreign policy deemed by many to be imperial. Most Christians do not self-identify with the Christian Right and its policies, especially progressive Christians and evangelicals in poorer churches and communities of color.[2] Many Christians, as well as people from other religious and secular traditions, object to the work of this one variant of Christianity and the kind of power it exercises in the administration of George W. Bush.

Why has this variant of Christianity attained the influence it has in the United States, and what is the nature of that power? Why do the Christians who claim not to support the militant variant nevertheless find themselves unable, or unwilling, to halt its influence? In responding to such questions, we cannot simply focus on the Christian Right, as much of the media has done.

The very term "Christian Right" can be confusing, especially if "right" is taken to mean generally "conservative." As will become clear in this book, the "Christian Right" is a subset of conservative Protestants in the U.S., one that adheres to and is committed to developing an aggressive U.S. American political romanticism. This tends to weld a Christian view of political history to new nationalist projects. Today's Christian Right, as I use the term, tends toward a program of political rule (some, as we shall see, explicitly embracing "theocracy"), which involves in our time the Christian Right's striking alliances with other nationalist groups (the "neoconservatives," for example, whom I discuss in depth below). The Christian Right is also developing strong support among big business and corporate funders.

It needs to be stressed, again, that many other conservative Protestants object to aspects of the Christian Right's agenda, as do, of course, the large number of progressive Protestants in white communities and across communities of color. Many who often self-identify as "evangelical" do not share the agenda, as is evidenced by the vigorous prophetic and progressive work of Jim Wallis in his best-selling book, *God's Politics*.[3] While the word "fundamentalist" is often used interchangeably with "the Christian Right," it too is problematic in that fundamentalists might and do often exhibit a kind of conservative Protestantism marked more by withdrawal from the world, and so would be uncomfortable with the more messianic and aggressive nationalism of the Christian Right.[4]

The term "Christian Right" is also problematic because it is often focused on as a kind of independent variable on the political scene today, the force driving the present politics of the Bush regime. This book seeks to be more measured. The militant, nationalist faith and moral agenda of the Christian Right is not the only post-9/11 power at work politically in the USA today. This book addresses the militant Christian Right as but one religious feature in the larger interplay of religion, politics, and U.S. imperial policy that congealed after the attacks on the Pentagon and World Trade Center on September 11, 2001. This will require a search for both historical and political perspective on that interplay.

This book argues that 9/11 is best interpreted as a "mythic moment" that temporarily ruptured the great myths of American Greatness by which many U.S. residents live. It explains how, amid that rupture, residents' fear and reactive patriotism enabled the resurgence, in culture and politics, of two powerful currents that long have run deep in U.S. history: American political romanticism and contractual liberalism, which have often produced and reinforced U.S. imperial dreaming and adventuring. That dreaming and adventuring is especially prevalent now in the post-9/11 USA., as many celebrate or debate the virtues of "American empire." Today's play of powers, mixing aggressive romanticism with a twisted liberalism that contracts out liberty and opportunity to a select few, has U.S. and global peoples under threat and in a most destructive moment.

Although I explore threats of destruction in our time, this book is also one of hope. There are still available to U.S. residents certain traditions that carry what I call "prophetic spirit." This is a tradition of spirit for all public life to which no religion has primary claim, and which those with secular commitments also help to create and sustain. The book traces the ways U.S. residents might work toward such a public tradition. In so doing, we might challenge the aggressive nationalisms of today's American political romanticism and the captivities and false promises of contractual liberalism.

Prophetic spirit, as I develop it here, can offer to U.S. residents a new appreciation of their land, a new sense of revolutionary belonging to a national project, without falling prey to the romanticisms and nationalisms bedeviling us today. Prophetic spirit can also enable a more radical liberalism that nurtures an enduring revolutionary expectation for the many, not just for a few.

I must note here my profound respect and gratitude for the work of Paul Tillich, whose 1933 work, *The Socialist Decision*, structures my experiment here by influencing the main categories I use in this book: American political romanticism, contractual liberalism, and prophetic spirit. Tillich, a philosopher, theologian, and analyst of culture and politics, wrote this work amid the rise to power of the Nazis during the Weimar Republic (1919– 1933). The work was confiscated and banned almost immediately by Nazi authorities. Later in his life, Tillich maintained that this was the work of which he was most proud. As several scholars today begin to reflect with rigor on the similarities between today's U.S. nationalism and destructive forms of nationalism in twentieth-century Europe, we must return to those who sought to think deeply while living through that period of turbulent conflicts.[5] Tillich was one of those who did precisely that. I have not used the same categories of political analysis that he did; Tillich wrote instead of "political romanticism," "bourgeois society," and "the socialist principle." Those terms do not work easily in the present U.S. context, and so I have renamed them and recast their dynamics. Yet the ways Tillich sorted out the interplay of religion and politics in relation to the barbarisms of nationalist power have been enormously instructive throughout this work. Scholars of Tillich's work will observe my obvious indebtedness and perhaps challenge my ways of relating him to the present struggle in the United States.

Permit me a word about this book's usage of the terms "America" and "American." While it seems that many throughout the world refer to the United States as "America," I continue to believe that this is an affront to all our neighbors to the North and to the South in this hemisphere who warrant the term as much as do U.S. residents. This is no matter of mere political correctness. To reserve the term exclusively to the United States, just one nation of the vast American hemisphere, tends to support linguistically the dominance that the U.S. has unjustly maintained over Latin American nations since its Monroe Doctrine.[6] When I write of "American romanticism," or "American empire," this will only be because those phenomena almost always presume the legitimacy of U.S. dominance in the Americas, and it is usually clear that I am criticizing those phenomena. At other times, when I am writing descriptively about the people of this most powerful nation, I will write of "the United States," "the U.S.," or simply "the USA."

It has not been easy for me to keep both dissent and hope alive in the recent years of U.S. war and imperial pursuit of what the Pentagon seeks for the U.S.: full-spectrum dominance (at home and abroad). What hope I have comes from movement work and organizing, carried on not only by indomitable Christian people in resistance, but also by those of other faith traditions and secular vision who carry on equally important work and struggle. None of these, nor any of those I thank below, are responsible for the flaws and limitations of this book.

I remain deeply grateful for the hope made by my activist colleagues at Princeton Theological Seminary, especially those who have risked speaking out publicly at our press conferences; at the seminary teach-ins against U.S. war, torture, and injustice; or in classes that I co-teach with them: Brian Blount, Nancy Duff, George Hunsinger, Stacy Johnson, Kathleen McVey, Peter J. Paris, Luis Rivera-Pagán, and Deborah Van Deusen Hunsinger. Princeton Seminary's new President, Dr. Iain Torrance, with his outspoken criticism of war, of U.S. outsourcing of torture to other countries—"the scandal of extraordinary rendition," as he named it in his 2005 inaugural address—inspires excellence in scholarship and moral practice. Princeton University colleagues such as Jeffrey Stout, Cornel West, Eddie Glaude, and others have been great exemplars of intellectual and moral virtue amid the challenge to reflect deeply on our times.

Activists of other faith traditions and secular vocations give me hope when it seems forthcoming from so few other places. In this regard, I thank those still at work in Educators for Mumia Abu-Jamal, the National Task Force for Mumia Abu-Jamal, Church

Folks for a Better America, the Catholic Workers, Middle Collegiate Church (New York City), and so many more.

Much of the research that lies behind this short book, and for other writings in progress, was made possible by a year-long international appointment in 2003–2004, at the Collegium for Advanced Studies at the University of Helsinki, Finland. The Collegium's scholars and the University of Helsinki teachers and staff all extended warm friendship, rigorous intellectual challenge, and research support of almost every kind.

I give special thanks to the 2005 doctoral student group at Princeton Theological Seminary—Tommy Casarez, Matthew Flemming, Elías Ortega-Aponte, Tabea Rösler, Laura Thelander, and Nimi Wariboko—who re-read Tillich's *The Socialist Decision* and also graciously discussed a version of this book with me.

Joe Herman's grace, skill, and efficiency at the computer keyboard were indispensable for the production of this text from the handwritten script I still prefer for book-writing in this digital age.

My daughters, Laura and Nadia, with their vigorous and fresh embrace of life and knowledge, teach me new things always and keep me alive with hope.

FAITH, AMERICAN EMPIRE, AND SPIRIT

"George W. Bush: Faith in the White House" proclaims the title of a 2004 video made by the Christian Right in the United States. It openly promotes George W. Bush's way of mixing Christianity with U.S. imperial governance.[1] The relation between religion and politics is always complex in important matters of governance, and some interplay almost always goes on, even when commitments exist to maintain walls for a separation of church and state. Today, however, among many with high positions in U.S. government, the militant version of Christian faith is vigorously infusing matters of national and international policy. It is as if faith with national power is now confirming many suspicions long held by faith's skeptics.

Is faith about ignorance? The Bush regime has stirred unprecedented numbers of scientists and scholars—twenty Nobel Laureates among them—to urge that the administration's "distortion of scientific knowledge for partisan political ends must cease."[2] Is faith prudish? Bush administration appointees drape cloths over barebreasted sculptures in the capitol city, as former Attorney General John Ashcroft did, and they censor government documents for explicit language about sex or healthy sexual expression.[3]

Is faith merely a spiritual cloak for usurping of political power? Members of the Bush regime deny it, but they nevertheless wax eloquent about taking down the wall between church and state, and include self-proclaimed theocrats like Robert Upton, of the Apostolic Congress, in high-level discussions at the White House.[4]

Is faith a dangerous substance that fuels religious warfare and rivalry? Again, Bush would say his faith is not dangerous. Yet when his undersecretary of defense (for intelligence) William Boykin invoked his Christian beliefs in public lectures to justify his battlefield exploits against a religiously demonized enemy whom he linked to the forces of Satan, the Bush regime did not publicly reprimand him or remove him from office.[5] In fact, millions of Christian believers, along with Bush himself, continually invoke Christian convictions in ways that cloak U.S. wars with a religious aura.

UNDER THE STAR OF EMPIRE—
POST-9/11 AMERICA'S IMPERIAL REGIME

The most troublesome feature of this militant faith, however, is its role in strengthening a post-9/11 imperial regime in America. It is certainly not the first time that Christian vision and U.S. imperial expansionism have collaborated. That collaboration has often showed itself in the history of the United States. The British Empire, too, has often grafted discourses about its people's divine mission to its practice of imperial vocation. As Walter Mignolo and others have argued, the earliest constructs of modernity and the "modern colonial world system" were driven by a sense of divine vocation and justified by religious rationales.[6]

Nevertheless, as I will explain below, the attacks of September 11, 2001 gave opportunity for a new interplay of powers that has enabled this militant Christian faith a vigorous entrée to power. Religious faith, especially the kind that is comfortable with aggressive national power and that follows theocratic instincts, tends to give to its government an unbridled sense of universal relevance and intensity of fervor. Both of these can quickly erode the very freedom and democracy that the faithful claim to defend with their rhetoric. Consider first the religious sense of universal import, which tends to feature a missionary consciousness that works unilaterally, envisioning the most important values to flow outward from the hallowed nation to others abroad. It also tends to devalue diversity of perspective on key human interests, overriding and running rough-shod over the critiques of others (abroad or at home) that are needed to hold governing elites accountable to the people they affect. Consider, too, intensity of religious fervor. In the government of a complex society, this often only makes worse the universalizing claims by eroding the more measured spirit of democratic deliberation that is needed for fostering conversation between citizens with rival claims and competing voices in the national and global context.

In the post-9/11 United States of America, the Christian Right's universalizing fervor seems to be giving nearly unqualified blessing for the nation's assumption of an imperial role in the world. These faithful join many others who either welcome or remain silent about the "star of empire" rising over this era of U.S. history. For many it is an occasion of national glory—a moment of triumph for a nation they already deem exceptional in its origins, its manifest destiny ever more confirmed, its protection and devotion more vital than ever. Pentagon planners and neoconservatives talk of "American Greatness," and right-wing Christian leaders urge a rebirth of American exceptionalism.

The star of empire, however, has effects that are hardly salutary in the world, especially not for the citizens of the imperial nation itself, as social theorist Emmanuel Todt has detailed in *After the Empire*.[7] As a simple heuristic device, the star of empire may be seen as a five-point star with each point dripping a poisonous bile into the body politic of the U.S., representing five ominous developments in U.S. social and political life that the post-9/11 imperial regime manifests.

UNILATERALISM

Since the fall of the Soviet Union, the U.S. has enjoyed single-superpower status and moved to enhance it in pursuit of what, even before 9/11, the Pentagon called "full spectrum dominance."[8] After 9/11, leaders have coalesced in a Bush regime committed to aggressive policy built explicitly on a unipolar view of the world in which the U.S. pursues its policies unilaterally. British historian Niall Ferguson argues persuasively that the U.S. *is* an empire but then less convincingly urges that the U.S. can use its imperial power as a liberal force.[9]

The invasion of Iraq in 2003 is but one dramatic example of U.S. unilateralism. To be sure, the U.S. holds consultations and conferences, and advances rhetoric about valuable allies and coalitions. These allies and coalitions, however, are rarely seen as real partners. The U.S. will court them occasionally, but basically the U.S. will do what it wills to do because it can. The ongoing assault on Iraq, as I will show below, was decided on by the U.S. without consultation and was launched without going back to the UN to get necessary approval. U.S. citizens should see this as ominous. To be the only superpower, to wield such great influence over the world's peoples *and* work in such a unilateralist fashion, stokes anger in citizens of the globe similar to that of many who are affected by a self-centered bully. A major result of unilateralism is the rise of global disrespect for the United States. Anti-American feelings run high in European countries, throughout "developing countries," and especially in the Arab world. In the long run, the people of the U.S. become isolated from the world and therefore more vulnerable. A government that is not respected leaves its people unprotected.

WAR

Bush's post-9/11 imperial regime has, in Shakespeare's famous phrase, "let slip the dogs of war." As Shakespeare also warned, it is the tendency of Caesar in imperial regimes to unleash war after crying "havoc!" The 9/11 event is still being pointed to as the havoc that makes U.S. wars necessary. The ominous, lamentable tragedy of these wars, especially of the unilateral and internationally illegal assault on Iraq, is registered in the tens of thousands of Iraqi civilian dead whom the U.S. government neither deigns to count nor cares to name. As of November 2004, the best studies project that Iraqi civilian dead since the 2003 invasion may be over 100,000, and find an Iraqi rate of death more than two times greater than the rate under Saddam Hussein before the invasion.[10] Even if this death rate recedes, and even if Iraqis and other citizens of Middle East nations find ways to forge fragile democratic forms in the crucible of war's destruction, the scars left by such a massively brutal assault will not foster the kind of dignity and freedom from fear needed to build lasting democracy. U.S. troops and their families have suffered greatly, too, with over 1,700 U.S. military personnel killed as of mid-2005, and thousands maimed for life.

The 9/11 moment was a dramatic media event, as have been the later U.S. war-making actions, thus increasing the tendency that all war has to shape our citizenry's everyday life. This perpetual war continually oozes bile into the body politic that, with time, can destroy much that U.S. residents claim to cherish. Chris Hedges, an experienced war correspondent, reminds us that "war forms its own culture." The ominous fact of the Bush regime's wars is that we all are steeped in a culture of war that "distorts memory, corrupts language and infects everything around it. . . ." "There is nothing redeeming about any war," Hedges continues, "including the supposed good wars that we might all agree had to be fought. . . . We must guard against the myth of war and the drug of war that can, together, render us as blind and callous as some of those we battle."[11]

NATIONALISM

For a long time U.S. citizens have had a strong sense of national identity, a sense of vocation that scholars have named "American exceptionalism."[12] After 9/11, for reasons I will examine in chapter 2, that exceptionalist sense—of being, for example, a special city on a hill, a light to the nations—was used in an almost desperate, self-congratulatory sense, letting loose what Anatol Lieven has called "the demons of radical nationalism."[13] This kind of nationalism puts a citizenry at risk because groups under its spell are those famously more ready to give up their liberties and to grant unchecked powers to national leaders that corrode democratic practice. Scholars debate the relative merits of nationalism for newly emergent states, but the nationalist currents running through the most powerful nation on earth are now inviting historical comparison with some of the destructive nationalist projects of European history, particularly those of Franco's Spain, Mussolini's Italy, Wilhelmine Germany before 1914, and those emergent in 1920s and 1930s Germany. We will explore the grounds for these comparisons in later chapters.

INEQUALITY

Both politically and economically, the Bush imperial regime has tolerated and reinforced inequality in the U.S. population. Economically, even before 9/11 and throughout the "roaring nineties," the gap of wages, income, and economic well-being between rich and poor widened greatly, receiving careful analysis by scholars like sociologist William Julius Wilson.[14] Amid the public trauma after 9/11, the Bush White House pushed through, with the support of the House of Representatives, legislation that would cut taxes for large corporations, taking advantage of a time when people were less willing to oppose the president. Bush also moved to cut individual income taxes, primarily for wealthy people, and later sought a rollback of the estate tax, which benefits the wealthiest sectors of U.S. society. In the first year of its second term, the Bush administration sought to privatize Social Security, again on the basis of cries of havoc regarding the health of future Social Security funds. Bankruptcy options for middle-class people laboring under credit-card debt were severely curtailed by proposed legislation of the Bush regime, while the bankruptcy options of wealthy elites were left intact.

Rising political inequality accompanies economic inequality, taking the form of eroded civil liberties for citizens and their ever-greater subordination to rulers' mandates and systems of surveillance. Notable here is the much-remarked USA PATRIOT Act, a massive omnibus surveillance and counter-terrorism bill rushed through Congress in October 2001, again in that post-9/11 atmosphere. It sweeps up a larger number of individuals and groups into the category of "terrorist," and authorizes more latitude for authorities to wiretap citizen communications and search private residences and offices. Of even more concern, perhaps, are the billions of dollars set aside to create a network of offices, agents, and surveillance systems that are now so diffused throughout government that just finding them is as difficult as monitoring them for abuses. The seriousness of the problem is noted not just by writers on the left such as Christian Parenti in his book *The Soft Cage*, but also by much more conservative minds like New Jersey judge and Fox News Senior Judicial Analyst Andrew Napolitano, who discusses in his book, *Constitutional Chaos*, government abuses, lying police throughout U.S. society, and also recent torture tactics at Guantánamo, Cuba.[15] Both of these sources document the tragic irony that, in the name of fighting an enemy who supposedly hates our freedom, as Bush has said, the U.S. government itself is taking away more and more of its own citizens' freedom.

TORTURE

The rise of empire's star in post-9/11 USA shows its brutal effectiveness by embracing the practice of torture. Torture is "any act by which severe pain or suffering, whether physical or mental, is intentionally inflicted by or at the instigation of a public official on a person for such purposes as obtaining from him or a third person information or confession, punishing him for an act he has committed, or intimidating him or other persons."[16] It is this definition, or versions similar to it, that makes torture prohibited by more than ten international and U.S. laws and conventions.[17]

The U.S. military has used torture in its covert and counterinsurgency campaigns abroad for decades. It has taught torture and admitted to writing manuals of torture.[18] Activists and populations throughout Latin America and the rest of the world know this well. A more than occasional ethos of torture has long characterized the treatment of prisoners in U.S. jails, prisons, immigrant detention centers, and police precinct stations. Thus, torture, as part of U.S. official policy, is nothing new.

Nevertheless, officials in the post-9/11 imperial regime have used citizen fear, nationalism, hyperpatriotism, and the culture of war to effect a still broader willingness to use torture and to permit a more aggressive policy of torture amid U.S. troop incursions into Iraqi homes, and at U.S.-guarded prison centers in Iraq, Afghanistan, and other locations around the world such as Guantánamo Bay Detention Center, Cuba, where the U.S. has housed more than 500 "illegal enemy combatants" who are denied human and civil rights and subjected to numerous abuses.[19] Even Michael Ratner, a seasoned international rights lawyer who has prosecuted many cases against U.S. officials for mistreatment of Haitians in Guantánamo and of Iraqi citizens suffering U.S. bombings and sanctions since 1991, has expressed a new level of shock at U.S. policies of abuse after 9/11, policies that include what he documents as "war crimes."[20] The abuses at Abu Ghraib, Iraq, and elsewhere, and the decisions of high-ranking officials like Secretary of Defense Donald Rumsfeld to relax rules to allow some forms of torture, is now stunningly on display in a host of essays and collected works, most notably in Karen Greenberg and Joshua Dratel's *The Torture Papers*.[21] Greenberg and Dratel also exhibit key memos seeking to justify torture techniques that were prepared by lawyer John Yoo and by White House Counsel Alberto Gonzales, who became Bush's second Attorney General. Page after page shows the emergent rationale for using torture in interrogations to get evidence wanted to fight terrorism. CIA official Cofer Black put it bluntly at a 2002 Senate Intelligence Committee hearing: "All you need to know is that there was a 'before 9/11' and there was an 'after 9/11'. After 9/11 the gloves come off."[22]

A major problem with this position is that in addition to being a flagrant violation of international law, a breach of the most basic of moral principles, and a disregard for the values of almost all religious traditions, torture rarely works. In fact, according to Dan Coleman, an experienced FBI interrogator who worked closely with the CIA on counterterrorism cases in the 1990s, it was the extending of due process to detainees that "made detainees more compliant, not less." Under torture and abuse, detainees will say anything, usually lies, and the truth becomes nearly impossible to sift out from the lies. "Brutalization doesn't work. We know that. Besides, you lose your soul."[23]

Torture, announced as a necessary practice and then implemented (even if sporadically), atomizes a citizenry and increases a state's capacity to rule without accountability. Here is where this point of empire's star oozes another poisonous bile into the body politic. Even if torture is only vaguely hinted at, the state's power to torture strengthens the state's power over its people. Torture is known to reduce the language of a tortured man to babbling sounds of his pre-speaking child. "He howls," notes Jacobo Timmerman, recalling his own and others' torture in Argentina.[24] Torture is the state's punishment of citizens' bodies. It is control over speech, and its haunting power erodes the communication among citizens that is necessary for collaboration in a democracy. Thus, as William Cavanaugh notes, "torture breaks down collective links and makes of its victims isolated monads."[25] Torture follows the first point of the star of empire in 9/11 USA, unipolar unilateralism, directly. Unilateral exercises of power can readily turn to torture, the ultimate expression of unilateral power played out on human bodies, reinforcing unilateral powers of the state.

A TRADITION OF PROPHETIC SPIRIT

Faith in the star of American empire rationalizes and affirms the imperial regime's unilateralism, war, nationalism, inequality, and even its policies of torture. It is that particular faith that many sense has a chokehold on the American populace today. The power of that militant faith, though, is not derived from the faith itself. It is supported by its alliances with other powers in the post-9/11 context, such as neoconservative policy makers and key forces in the corporate world. These other powers will also be analyzed in this text, but amid that analysis this book will increasingly highlight a different kind of faith, "prophetic spirit." More accurately, it is another tradition, one that is often hidden and fluid. I call it a "tra-dition" because it has a distinctive social character, which I will try to delineate, and it has a substantial historical legacy. It is impor-tant to bring this tradition to the fore, to identify it, think it, and take up its practices, especially in post-9/11 USA. Although this book will develop the idea of prophetic spirit largely as a resource for resisting the massive imperial reconfiguration going on in the United States, it will also make it clear that prophetic spirit is just as important for resisting other forms of injustice such as racism, patriarchal and sexual violence, and more.

Although fully articulating what I mean by "prophetic spirit" will require the entire book's unfolding, at this point, I would say that it is a resource for resisting, challenging, and counter-ing not only the pious nationalism of the Christian Right that does obeisance to empire, but also the other cultural, political, and economic dynamics of empire in the U.S. *Prophetic spirit is a cultural political current that uses mythic languages, art, and political practices to create justice and peace for the weak, for the marginalized and oppressed without whose emancipation the whole body politic lives in travail.* Prophetic spirit is not just belief against the odds posed by a powerful empire. Nor is it only individuals' courage of speak-ing truth to power in the name of justice for the weak and the poor. Prophetic spirit is a persistent, insurgent tradition that carries and generates new social practices needed in this post-9/11 imperial moment. Prophetic spirit is a revolutionary tradi-tion that persists today, a legacy that helped generate the United States at its founding but that was generally betrayed, as we shall see, by its founders.

"Prophetic spirit" sounds religious. Indeed, the origin and meanings of the term emerge from major religious traditions, especially Jewish ones, but also from Christianity and Islam. Religious traditions, however, have no monopoly on the pro-phetic function. Being *prophetic*, "speaking before" others, espe-cially speaking to the powerful who damage and oppress the public life we seek to build together, is a function that can be shared by many outside and inside the religious traditions. True, the Hebrew term that is usually translated as "prophet," *navi'*, and its derivatives, has almost always been bound up with a sense of divine calling and commission; but so also were other figures (priests, manics, magicians). The distinguishing human feature of the Hebrew prophets' work, which marked their hearers' relation to the divine, was social criticism: discernments and warnings about trends in the collective life of their people. The prophet Ezekiel, for example, understood himself as a "sentinel" warning "the house of Israel."[26]

Secular traditions of intellectual life and politics can also carry this prophetic function, often doing better than the religious faithful, especially when groups such as the Christian Right commandeer the public witness of religions and make common cause with the power-builders of nationalism and empire. Religious ethicist Jeffrey Stout suggests that the tone of many secular critics today "can be traced back to the Romantic transformation of biblical prophecy into a secular vocation of social criticism."[27] Whether this secular vocation is traceable largely to biblical prophecy or drinks deeply, also, from its own independent sources of social criticism (for example, reason and humanism) as Susan Jacoby argues in her book, *Freethinkers: A History of American Secularism,* is an issue that I cannot settle in this book.[28] It is significant enough to note that key practices of prophetic spirit can be pursued by both religious and secular social critics. Prophetic spirit can galvanize many from the world religious systems, from movements of indigenous and other global spiritualities, and from the various kinds of organized movements to renew popular democracy.

Prophetic spirit's historical roots in major religious traditions give it a spiritual character that persists even when it becomes a tradition in which secular as well as religious social critics find some shared perspective. But this spiritual character does not mean that secular and religious participants in prophetic spirit share in the beliefs, rituals, or organizational life proper to explicitly religious practices and systems. What they do share is a spiritual character, an integrating and animating power that conveys a pervasive frame of meaning for individual and collective life.[29]

In this sense, the militant faith of today's Christian Right also has a spiritual character, but it is markedly different from that of prophetic spirit. This book draws that difference in high relief, showing how, even amid post-9/11 cultural and political powers, prophetic spirit can birth alternative ways of valuing the past and future of the U.S. national project.

The "founding fathers" of the United States imbibed some revolutionary orientations from people with prophetic spirit who, across the seventeenth and eighteenth centuries, were displaced by, but resisted, the rise of modern European capitalism, who struggled to abolish slavery, who contested forced impressments into the transoceanic ship culture of empires, and who organized rebellions in major ports around the rim of the Atlantic. The likes of Samuel Adams, Thomas Jefferson, James Madison, and others followed reports of this revolutionary spirit, tapping into its tradition but then placing a cap on it. That slavery, declaring slaves to be but three-fifths human in spite of fervent cries for abolition at that time, was enshrined in the U.S. Constitution, is exemplary of the founders' ways of limiting the drives toward revolutionary emancipation.

Ever since this nation's founding, and in sundry ways, U.S. peoples have been locked in a struggle between the revolutionary spirit of the multinational, multiracial traditions that have made possible the U.S. national experiment in democracy and the counter-revolutionary ethos and regimes holding back that spirit. All too many U.S. administrations have followed the founding fathers' "tapping and capping" strategy: tapping into the enlivening and liberating power of peoples' movements for change and then capping that power so as to keep national policies in what amounts to a counter-revolutionary ethos in which U.S. citizens' talk about their ideals becomes ever more hollow.

Prophetic spirit might be developed to take on the imperial regime of today as it has taken on, survived, and at times subverted the counter-revolutionary forces of times past. Today's post-9/11 imperial regime is one of those counter-revolutionary forces, and, as in the past, prophetic spirit haunts it.

SPECTERS OF EMPIRE

Prophetic spirit is a specter haunting U.S. empire today. Empire must corral, co-opt, or repress prophetic spirit in order to safeguard its imperial projects. Why this is so will become clear as this book details the qualities of prophetic spirit in later chapters. I emphasize here that prophetic spirit is not in conflict simply with today's U.S. imperial regime—with its unilateralist projects, its war, nationalism, inequality, and torture. Indeed it is true, bearers of prophetic spirit challenge the specific features of imperial formation in any era, but it is even more important for prophetic spirit to be a force that critically engages and challenges other cultural-political currents that also help to produce U.S. imperial aggrandizement. Again, to challenge U.S. empire sufficiently it is never adequate to think only in terms of imperial states and politics. One must also focus on distortions created by white racism, patriarchal and heterosexist structures, capitalist exploitation, and other dynamics. Prophetic spirit is marked by a way of being that broadens and deepens our discernment, that keeps to the fore this struggle against a multiplicity of unjust structures.

This book will foreground two rival traditions that produce and sustain U.S. imperial regimes and that opportunistically strengthened themselves by using the 9/11 moment: American romanticism and contractual liberalism. Each of these traditions is carried in cultural-political currents that extend throughout U.S. history, reaching back into eras that antedate the U.S. founding. Prophetic spirit must engage, challenge, and overcome those deep-running currents in U.S. social life today if it is going to overcome today's most recent U.S. imperial manifestation.[30]

By using the word "specter" I am not referring to powers from some ghostly realm of phantasms; I discuss specters in the more historical sense as forces, imagined or expected, that can develop in history and society and have consequences that are dangerous for some but fulfilling for others. With this sense in mind, the book's treatment of religion and politics is a story of three specters. First, the *specter to empire,* prophetic spirit, haunts and seeks to emancipate peoples within and without the United States from the burdens imposed by its new empire. Prophetic spirit is a danger to imperial formation. Then there are the other two specters, the *specters of empire,* the specter of American romanticism, and that of contractual liberalism. These are the specters against which prophetic spirit must labor if it is to resist imperial regimes in more lasting and effective ways. To understand the rise of the U.S. imperial regime after 9/11, these two specters must be understood both historically and in their present configurations. As I will show, as specters, these two traditions carry certain dangers for the health of the U.S. body politic. Prophetic spirit is a specter to empire by the way it engages and challenges the specters that so often foster empire in America.

PLAN OF THE BOOK

This book on prophetic spirit begins with two chapters seeking to discern the character and dynamics of our times. Chapter 1 offers some guideposts for thinking about evil in public life, acknowledging that so many U.S. citizens in post-9/11 USA now claim to be facing evil in new ways and so have become vulnerable to their leaders' simplistic talk of battles between the forces of good and those of the "evil" ones, the "terrorists." Prophetic spirit must begin with a more sophisticated understanding of the evil we face as well as the evil we do.

Chapter 2, "The 9/11 Moment," offers a reading of the evil many U.S. citizens believe they suffered on September 11, 2001. I argue that 9/11 ushered in not so much a new historic moment but more a new *mythic* moment for U.S. citizens' understanding of their nation. The 9/11 moment ruptured many Americans' conscious and unconscious senses of being an exceptionalist nation in the world. A surprise attack of sudden destruction shattered the illusions of many that the U.S. homeland was an exceptional site, the protected home of a people pursuing their manifest destiny. Exceptionalist confidence was replaced with heightened fear

and nostalgia. The hyperpatriotism surfacing since 9/11 marks
the emergence of a new nationalism in which citizens seek desper-
ately to recapture and restore the confidences of the exceptionalist
myth. In times like the 9/11 moment, as evidenced by the histories of nationalism in twentieth-century Europe and elsewhere,
such citizens are uniquely susceptible to being tyrannized at home
and pressed into service for imperial adventuring abroad.

Chapter 3, "The Specter of American Romanticism," begins
the historical and political theory of the book. It treats post-9/11
citizens in the U.S. as engaged in a crisis of belonging, a crisis
that has, even before our nation's founding, often driven people to
embrace an American political romanticism. Pervading the fur-
thest reaches of their vision and the deepest places of many U.S.
citizens' being is a tendency to romance and to revere their country's origins. This chapter, therefore, will view the crises of post-
9/11 USA as a crisis of what I call "belonging being"—a sense of
connection to heritage and place, to a revered group history and
shared land. If the work of prophetic spirit in the present moment
is to be effective, it will need to acknowledge peoples' needs for
belonging because it is these needs that now are spoken to, galvanized and exploited by the Christian Right (religious romanticists) and by the neoconservatives (usually secular romanticists),
both of whom are discussed in this chapter.

Chapter 4, "The Specter of Contractual Liberalism," will make
clear that post-9/11 America must also be seen in relation to
another cultural-political current that is interwoven with American romanticism. This current arises from another human feature that is expressed in politics: the drive and demand for the
new—for growth, restoration, healing, enriched flourishing.
This is what I call "expectant being." Today, however, a complex
corporatist class structure in the U.S.—what Michael Lind refers
to it as a "white overclass"[31]—keeps expectant being and its liberal projects ever frustrated, bracing against the walls set up by
class, race, gender, and other patterns of exclusion. I will detail
in this fourth chapter how contractual liberalism has so distorted
liberal traditions that they are being transformed into an outright
anti-liberal modernism.

Chapter 5, "The Specter of Prophetic Spirit," gives prophetic spirit a more explicit and extensive treatment. In the context of the post-9/11 USA, prophetic spirit must acknowledge, critique, and go beyond the ways that the specters of American romanticism and contractual liberalism haunt the U.S. body politic with imperial tendencies. Prophetic spirit, while saying no to the distortions and destruction of American romanticism and contractual liberalism, nevertheless offers a new kind of belonging being and sets new terms for "expectant being." Here I also clarify why the way of the prophetic is a way of spirit. In chapter 6, "Revolutionary Belonging," I explain how prophetic spirit points toward alternative traditions for belonging being (with fresh histories, stories, and myths of its own) to rival the recurrent nationalist myths of American romanticism. Chapter 7, "Revolutionary Expectation," then unfolds prophetic spirit's distinctive way of embracing expectant being by advocating and working for a radical liberalism. Radical liberalism is how prophetic spirit breaks the strangleholds of the exploitative market economies that carry the specter of contractual liberalism. Thus, prophetic spirit not only offers a new myth of origins to counter American romanticism, it also seeks to free American liberalism from its contractual and corporatist captivity. Prophetic spirit thus prepares the way for a new orientation toward religious and cultural practices in the U.S. after 9/11.

1

EVIL IN PUBLIC LIFE TODAY

For us, terrorism remains the great evil of our time, and
the war against this evil, our generation's greatest cause.

—DAVID FRUM AND RICHARD PERLE, *AN END TO EVIL*

How are we to think about evil in public life today? There is
no way that this single chapter can even begin to respond fully to
the notorious theological problem of evil. (How can evil coexist with an allegedly all-powerful, good God? Why do bad things
happen to good people?) Instead, the emphasis of this chapter is
prompted by the frequent talk about evil in United States public
life today, especially after the 9/11 attacks on the World Trade
Center and Pentagon in 2001, and particularly by U.S. policy
makers. In this chapter, I want to foreground today's public rhetoric of evil and emphasize how a different approach to evil guides
the rest of this book.

A DOMINANT RHETORIC OF EVIL

The quote at the beginning of this chapter by David Frum and
Richard Perle—both resident fellows of the powerful conservative think tank the American Enterprise Institute—displays the
basic logic of today's public rhetoric of evil. Frum was also a special assistant to George W. Bush, and Perle was chairman of the
Defense Policy Board during Bush's first presidential term. Three
major themes usually interplay in this public rhetoric. First, terrorism—understood as sudden attacks against the U.S. at home

or abroad that take a toll on civilian life or military personnel—is announced as the great evil. Then, second, the U.S. public and its policymakers are called to set themselves "against" the great evil. Finally, the being of the whole nation is interpreted in terms of commitment to a cause against evil that is seen as defining "our time."

Through the U.S. mainstream media especially, each of these rhetorical themes is placed before citizens with great drama, accenting citizens' sacrifice, determination, and courage. Each theme, though, represents a simplistic narrowing of vision. In the first theme, "the great evil" tends to be exhausted by whatever one's fears and interests construct as terrorism, short-circuiting sustained public attention to other kinds of evil (the waging of war, lack of health-care provisions for a citizenry, racism, institutionalized discrimination against women, climate change, and so on) or to the conditions generating evil. In the second, vision is narrowed largely to what we are fighting *against,* giving little critical attention to what it is we might be fighting or living *for.* And in the third theme, the whole nature of "our time" tends to be reduced to this war against terrorism, while federal deficits and environmental pollution, for example, are placed down the list of concerns of our time.

To be sure, there is not a complete absence of talk about the public virtues being fought for, but in national politics and mainstream media these virtues tend to be restricted to nationalist mantras about "our freedom": the terrorists hate "our freedom"; citizens must "defend liberty." This public rhetoric of evil brings into motion today a long-running tradition that ethicist Peter Singer has discussed as an "American Manichaean tradition,"[1] named after dualistic cosmologies and religious visions that put evil and good into radical opposition, and often also see the good as under unrelenting attack by invading evil.[2] The result tends to be that the American goods (democracy, freedom, or whatever else) seem to have little of their own distinctive, proactive force beyond the actions of tightening security against the next attack, curtailing civil liberties, plugging holes in the borders, or worse, aping "the great evil's" tactics through ever-increasing brutality, torture, and war. The curtailment of freedom at home and the fanatic exercise of new levels of brutality abroad in Iraq, for example, evidence how today's rhetoric of evil exhibits, in fact, a lack of confidence in the American goods, a failure to see American virtues as fresh, vital, lively forces with transformable power and appeal in themselves. Instead, the good is largely something to be protected, armor-plated from external evil.

THE "JUST WAR AGAINST TERROR" SCHOLARS

This dominant public rhetoric of evil exists in a more complex form in the team of U.S. scholars who released a statement, "What We're Fighting For—A Letter from America," to the world press in February 2002. Well-known figures among the letter's sixty signers included James Q. Wilson, Amitai Etzioni, Francis Fukuyama, Os Guiness, Samuel Huntington, Glenn C. Loury, Richard J. Mouw, Michael Novak, John Witte Jr., Max L. Stackhouse, and Michael Walzer. It was published toward the end of the first U.S. bombing campaign against the Taliban in Afghanistan.[3] The statement featured University of Chicago ethicist Jean Bethke Elshtain as its primary drafter, and she later appended the statement to her book-long rationale, *Just War against Terror: The Burden of American Power in a Violent World*. While the statement was disseminated in 2002, Elshtain's book came out in 2003, while the U.S. assault in Iraq was well underway. It is difficult not to see the book as an argument for both the Afghanistan and Iraq campaigns, sites of conflict where the author and signers see just war criteria being applied by U.S. military forces. True, at least one signer, Francis Fukuyama, has raised serious questions about the campaign in Iraq, even referring to it as "a mistake."[4] Also, in November 2002 Fukuyama, Elshtain, Stackhouse, and others issued a clarifying memorandum about certain pre-emptive policies of the Bush administration in Iraq that showed tendencies to violate criteria of just war.[5]

This chapter focuses substantively on the "Letter from America" that Elshtain drafted for sixty signatures, and on her book, for two reasons. First, the "Letter" encapsulates in purportedly scholarly fashion some of the main features of the public rhetoric of evil prevailing today. Second, because her book was warmly received and praised by many major media outlets and reviewers,[6] being selected by *Publishers Weekly* as "One of the Best Non-Fiction Books of 2003," allowance needs to be made for a more critical examination at this time.

Apparently, these "violations" of just war criteria that Elshtain and the co-signers began to discern after writing their letter forced them to consider the worlds of power in which criteria and principles are implemented and affected by interests and distortion. Their earlier "Letter from America," and Elshtain's book as a whole, tended to be formalistic and intellectualistic, claiming a virtuous advantage for their positions, justifying the war against terrorism on the basis of formal principles. Many might agree—as, in fact, even many Saudi scholars did—that the general principles announced at the beginning of the Letter are worthy ones, even basic human values shared by all peoples.[7] But suspicion of the United States' right to wage war today is due not so much to disagreement about announced principles, but to debate about the ways the U.S. has historically manifested its political compliance or noncompliance with those principles, a historical performance that is hardly honorable as examples below will show.

Consider how Elshtain and her co-signers announce that they, representing the United States, are fighting for an ideal holding that "most disagreements about values call for civility, openness to others' views, and reasonable argument in pursuit of truth."[8] Can it really be said that this ideal is, or was, one of the "founding ideals" that "most define our way of life," when a history of vigorous racism at the U.S. founding, especially against Native and African Americans, often licensed discriminatory brutality?[9] Moreover, in the present, regarding the Middle East, in spite of real progress on some fronts, the U.S. has yet to practice the kind of "civility" or "openness to other views" that places a priority on supporting democratic movements organized by Arab peoples themselves, especially if those peoples challenge U.S. geopolitical or oil-extraction interests. U.S. "openness" in the Middle East has almost always meant placing U.S. control over the flow and cost of oil and gas resources in those regions over and above promoting democracy and human rights for the citizens of Arab nations.[10] U.S. policies with Saudi Arabia are only the most clear of many possible examples.[11] Absent that modicum of openness, in what sense can it seriously be maintained that civility is one of the convictions that "most define our way of life"?

Such questions can be posed relative to multiple sites on every continent. The U.S. tolerated and supported the Duvalier dictatorships in Haiti, helped maintain the Somoza dictatorships in Nicaragua, serviced the juntas in Guatemala and Argentina,[12] and cleared the way for the dictatorship of Augusto Pinochet after the overthrow of Salvador Allende in Chile on September 11, 1973.[13] In Asia, Indonesia is just one site where U.S. covert and CIA action is a matter of established record, and where torture and counter-insurgency campaigns have resulted in thousands of deaths.[14] Nor has the U.S. been a supporter of effective and independent democratic growth in Africa, as the example of the Congo, whose economy the U.S. helped bridle almost from its beginning, demonstrates.[15] For years the U.S. along with Britain failed to support Nelson Mandela in his struggle against apartheid in South Africa and were invested in maintaining the repressive regime there.[16] Greece? Spain?[17] These latter are sites around the edge of Europe where key elements of U.S. national power also have been at work to deadly effect, often violating the list of founding ideals that Elshtain and her co-signers claim they are fighting for when the U.S. wages war.

Let us admit that developing moral judgments regarding U.S. covert and overt abuses in each cultural and historical location— even when they generate, as many have, genocidal impact—is always a complex matter.[18] But the evidence is clear that U.S. leaders have routinely, systemically abused U.S. power and looked away from cases of genocide that they could have taken steps to help prevent.[19] Today, when the U.S. occupies the role of sole superpower, it is not unreasonable for many citizens—at home and abroad—to be suspicious that U.S. abuses will persist or increase. Elshtain and her signers do admit in their "Letter from America" that mistakes have been made and that the line between good and evil "runs through the middle of every human heart."[20] But they do not carefully examine the line of repression of other nations that runs through U.S. history. They rarely consider seriously the fact that less-than-ideal or abusive intentions just might be at work in today's war campaigns and occupations by the U.S. in Afghanistan and Iraq. Any such suspicions are dismissed as naïve conspiracy theory. To the contrary, activists who oppose those military adventures, including family members of the victims of the 9/11 attacks, are people who know the real costs of war and who also know the propensity of the U.S. to use military violence against others for its own interests, as it has so often in the past.

I have provided the above careful documentation of previous systemic U.S. abuse of international power because Elshtain's performance in her book, like many in the mainstream media today, deploys a kind of swashbuckling discourse that portrays critics of U.S. war as "anti-American" or as "naïve pacifists" deploying specious arguments and false analogies without evidence. The "Letter from America"—its intellectual content and discursive style—is marked by a studied avoidance of critique of abusive U.S. policies abroad. As to content, the avoidance is evident in an intellectual formalism that announces U.S. ideals without studying the history of success *and* failure to manifest those ideals in practice. Elshtain's dismissive tendency is especially evident in her refusal to examine Noam Chomsky's analysis of 9/11 and U.S. hegemony "because analyzing it is like shooting fish in a barrel—it just isn't very interesting."[21] Elshtain writes as if a rigorously argued literature on U.S. imperialism did not exist.[22]

What this means is that Elshtain and the "just war against terror" scholars offer little more than a sophisticated version of today's public rhetoric of evil, which is rooted in American Manichaeism. In other words, they position the U.S. as the good nation whose life and being is threatened by opposing evil, "terrorism," with little care to attend to its own entailment in atrocity and terror. We might note as well that Elshtain's very book title tilts toward a Manichaeism that takes as adversary in this "just war" not just movements of brutal people in al-Qaeda ("terrorists"), but the ever more general, almost metaphysically ubiquitous "terror." Her arguments crystallize around a pervasive viewpoint that the terrorist attacks on the World Trade Center and the Pentagon grew out of "implacable hatred that . . . mystifies us."[23] This Manichaean formula is also evident in the great agency she gives to terrorist actions, rooting them largely in Osama bin Laden's "depth of hatred." Moreover, she tends to abstain from considering terrorist actions in relation to other recurring actions in political or social life (especially in the actions of the U.S.). As she says, "This depth of hatred does not grow out of any specific action or lack of action, on the part of those who are its target."[24] Thus Elshtain avoids acknowledging that, after the bombing of the World Trade Center in 1993, several scholars had made clear that this edifice was a symbol of power, attracting the disgruntled rage of some groups. Mark Juergensmeyer, for example, wrote in 2000, "The towers are in their own way as American as the Statue of Liberty or the Washington Monument, and by assaulting them activists put their mark on a visibly American symbol."[25] Rather than factor these matters into her analysis, Elshtain stays within the Manichaean frame, recycling what the public rhetoric of evil usually repeats: "An implacable hatred is targeting us and we must stop it. It is just to do so." She can even embrace the rhetoric of evil promoted by officials of the Bush administration, who reduce "implacable evil's" attacks to its alleged hatred of "our freedom." About Islamists, not distinguishing between the violence-prone and other Islamists,[26] she states emphatically, "They loathe us because of who we are and what our society represents."[27] Or again, "It is freedom itself that they despise."[28]

ON UNDERSTANDING TERRORISM AS EVIL

We try to give evil depth with our explanations. But it
just keeps spreading. That is why we must stop it: So
that the good might be revealed before us.[29]

—JEAN BETHKE ELSHTAIN

Elshtain is certainly correct that explanations of evil are not in themselves a force sufficient to stop evil. But in her statement above, and throughout her book, she suggests that explanatory accounts of evil are irrelevant to stopping evil and, further, that when one seeks explanations one is uninterested in stopping it. This shows another feature of the post-9/11 public rhetoric of evil: the denigration of explanations and attempts to understand terrorist attacks.

Let me provide an example from my own experience of public debate after 9/11. In the opening week of the U.S. bombing campaign in Afghanistan, I wrote an op-ed in the *Newark Star Ledger*.[30] I was pleased to have found a way, in October 2001, to publish an alternative voice to the war hysteria, its superpatriotism, and the wanted-dead-or-alive tough talk then being propounded by the Bush regime. I had called the essay "Being Safe in the USA," urging that the U.S. consider its exploitative international policies (in the Middle East, Latin America, and elsewhere) as at least one cause of the conditions that breed terrorist actions, especially among a brutal few who are most likely to attack symbols of power like the World Trade Center and the Pentagon.

The reactions were not unexpected. The newspaper itself framed my op-ed in the more simplistic logics of the day, changing its title to the more incendiary, "We Can Trace Roots of Terror to Ourselves." The next day the paper's chief conservative columnist wrote a special piece attacking the "root cause" analysts like me, whom he had expected to "come out of their caves." Of course, in spite of the twice-stated caveat in my essay that to try *to understand* the conditions of evil is not *to justify* it, my critic simply claimed the contrary about me. Some later letters to the editor appreciated the viewpoint I tried to express. The bulk of the letters, however, resisted any call to "understanding." The attacks, in the minds of all but a few, could be thought of only as unconditional evil. The Manichaean spirit triumphed again.

This public reaction is predictable in a climate of public fear after 9/11 and when a regime in power is allowed to make nearly all dissent look inappropriate. Part of stifling dissent is disparaging efforts to explain conditions giving rise to evil actions. I encountered this tendency again at an April 2002 conference at the University of Chicago, where I was delivering a major paper on Christian theological responses to terrorism. The paper was receiving some good challenge and critique from my designated interlocutor when the moderator of the event, who happened to be Jean Bethke Elshtain, interrupted with "Well, Mark, what country *would* you like to live in?" This love-it-or-leave-it retort is rooted in the assumption that thoroughgoing critique of one's government somehow disqualifies one from belonging or wanting to belong to this country. In responding to Elshtain, I first mused internally about the many other countries I could appreciate living in, having lived in or visited for short times (Mexico, Guatemala, Finland, Spain), but then, more wisely, asserted my abiding right and desire to live here, to dissent and seek transformation of this land. Elshtain's resistance to dissenting understanding, her frequent portrayal of it as an appeasing, soft way to deal with the radical evil of terrorism today, is consistent with the rhetoric of evil that we noted above as characterizing the "just war against terror" scholars.

More seriously, Elshtain is also engaged in a misreading of some of the twentieth century's great theologians, molding them into service of her own post-9/11 affirmation of a war on terror. This is especially notable regarding her interpretation of the German émigré and prominent U.S. theologian Paul Tillich, who forged a professional life in the U.S. from 1933 to 1965 after fleeing his native country during the Nazi rise to power. Tillich, who also had seen the evil of war in the trenches of World War I and who vigorously organized against and criticized encroaching power of national socialism during the Weimar Republic in Germany, worked for a religious socialism and was widely known for his work as a radical theologian.[31] His 1933 book, *The Socialist Decision*, was banned almost immediately by the Nazis.

Elshtain, in *Just War against Terror*, exalts Tillich, lamenting there are not more like him. She focuses exclusively on the Tillich of the radio addresses he was commissioned to give for the Voice of America programs aired in Germany in the 1940s.[32] Elshtain portrays Tillich as among those who "did not equivocate, exculpate or 'understand' to the point of losing their own dignity as human subjects. Evil is that which diminishes."[33] She is certainly right that Tillich did not equivocate or exculpate in his critiques of Nazism (and, in fact, he supported the use of violence against his own country in World War II). Nevertheless, with her statement she evokes a public impatience that does not want to "understand" terrorism, simultaneously masking how Tillich in fact did seek to understand evil, even to the point of criticizing the nations which suffered Nazi terror. Moreover, by placing the word *understand* inside quotation marks, she makes an intentional jab at those who plead in our time for an understanding of the evil of terrorism and for limits to retaliatory, Manichaean practices today. In so doing, Elshtain suggests that Tillich is a voice that knows, like she does, that evil is just an "implacable hatred" that must be opposed, focused in a "Hitler or a Stalin or a bin Laden."[34]

This, however, is a departure from Tillich's understanding. Even in his wartime radio addresses, he refused to focus only on the implacable hatred of one man or of one group. Barbarism in Germany, as he named it and anticipated it rightly, was significantly also the result of forces coursing through almost all realms of society, realms that allowed Hitler and the Nazis to lead the country. He thus could criticize intellectuals in realms of art, science, and literature, as well as landed proprietors and large entrepreneurs in Europe. These latter economically respectable sectors, he noted, "handed over weapons and capital to National Socialism." He also stressed that a great portion of "German writers, scholars and artists" who made "common cause with the forces of reaction, which held the stirrups" for the Nazi regime, bear significant amounts of responsibility.[35]

In the same year he wrote these words to his German audience, he was telling U.S. audiences, "Nobody should attribute our period of world wars and world revolutions to the accident of a special national character, for instance, of the Russian or the German or the Japanese character, or to dictatorial leaders, such as Stalin or Hitler, whose rise to power is even more accidental."[36] During the war, he advocated what he termed a "theory of structural necessity" and examined structural trends, the deterministic forces shaping the centuries, especially through the energies of capitalist society.[37]

Tillich had a sense of tragic complexity about the rise of Hitler that was born out of a willingness to examine structural conditions, even to the point of radically criticizing the allied Western powers he supported in the fight against Nazism. Unlike Elshtain—and this is what makes her misrepresentation of Tillich so egregious—Tillich worked well beyond the limitations of the public rhetoric of evil that we see today in the United States. Tillich's alternative spirit of critique in the face of evil is evident in the following striking questions, which he put to an audience in Indianapolis in the midst of World War II, an era when Japan and Hitler's Germany were often positioned as implacable evil.

> Let me finish with three questions by which our attitude to the meaning of this war can be tested.
>
> When we fight in Japan, do we fight a racial war, a war for the maintenance of European imperialism in Asia, or do we fight for the freedom of Asia also from ourselves?
>
> When we fight on the side of Russia, do we fight on her side because it is useful for us to do so for the time being, but with the intention of excluding her once more from European affairs, or do we acknowledge seriously her right to determine, on an equal basis with the Western nations, the destiny of Europe and Asia?
>
> When we fight in Europe, do we go as punishers, educators, cultural and economic conquerors in order to actualize the "American Century," or do we go in order to help Europe to survive and to be re-established in new forms and for a new future?[38]

Willingness to pose these kinds of questions, to seek this kind of understanding, is rooted in a fundamentally different approach to evil than the largely Manichaean form of the present. Many religions have a critique of Manichaean, or dualist, views of evil.[39] The next section in this chapter will remind us of some of Christianity's own very basic teachings on evil. They are important because they give rise to the alternative spirit for critique of evil that we see in Tillich, which will guide the remainder of this book.

EVIL AS DISTORTION OF THE GOOD

Elshtain's reluctance to examine the ambiguities and failings of European and U.S. modernity, especially when examining the evil of the present post-9/11 moment, and her departure from the example Tillich set when he criticized the economic and political trends running through capitalism and many sectors of European societies, may be traced to the way she reads fifth-century Christian theologian St. Augustine on evil. Elshtain even blends a misreading of Augustine's position on evil with the current resurgence of American Manichaeism. "As St. Augustine taught," she says in a paraphrase of him without quoting him, "evil is a turning of one's back on the good. It is a depletion. It cannot generate. It can only destroy."[40] Indeed, this element does appear in Augustine, and some Manichaean traits, as well as egregious hierarchies, pervade Augustine's writings, but on the matter of good and evil, a much more prominent notion than the kind of opposition that Elshtain sees is his view that evil is bound up *with* the good, that habits buried in the good delight of human beings in history are what generate evil and give it its force. Evil often latches on to whatever humans delight in, take as good.[41] Evil for Augustine becomes a generative, creative power in history by exploiting its parasitic relationship with the good. Especially the mature Augustine argued in this vein. Peter Brown, after carefully examining Augustine's doctrinal texts and several sermons on the matter, described his middle age of *tolerantia* and *patientia* in this way: "It is as if a mist had suddenly descended on Augustine's landscape, blurring the obvious contours of good and bad."[42]

So, even if Augustine defines evil as a "privation of the good," this does not warrant Elshtain's Manichaean-like oppositionalism of "evil versus the good." (A *privation* is the loss or absence of something that is normally, or should be, present.) It is deprivation, yes, but as privation *of* the good. If we really wish to stop evil, we need to grapple as Augustine did with the frequent, mutual coinherence of evil with good. In a passage that is almost as close as Augustine gets to identifying a "cause" of evil, he points

to "a defection *from* the good."[43] Remembering Augustine's awareness of the mutual interplay of evil with the good is especially crucial if, under the pressure of the 9/11 attacks, U.S. citizens are
to avoid transforming their civic virtues into civically destructive
vices.

Let us recall more simply some of the basic aspects of evil that
are familiar from the New Testament, some of which inform elements in Augustine's more complex views. These reinforce the
necessity to examine evil as a privation of the good, of considering evil and good together. Two of these aspects are particularly important in the New Testament. Both are the seeds of later
Christian theologians' critique of the Manichaean rhetoric of
evil.[44]

OPPORTUNISTIC EVIL

The first aspect is that evil—especially the human form of moral
evil that is called "sin"—exists in both the allegedly righteous and
allegedly unrighteous. This is often forgotten by those who count
themselves "good" or "righteous," over and against those deemed
"evil" or "unrighteous." A well-known admonition of Jesus pre-
sumes this: "How can you say to your neighbor, 'Let me take the
speck out of your eye,' while the log is in your own eye. You hyp-
ocrite, first take the log out of your own eye, and then you will
see clearly to take the speck out of your neighbor's eye" (Matt
7:4-5). Evil is rarely something static or lodged in an individual
or social group. It is always on the move, capable of residing any-
where. Popular writer Lance Morrow, a *Time* magazine columnist and Boston University professor, remarked wisely on evil's
"fungus quality" in a recent meditation on evil: "Do not bother
to demonize people as being inherently evil. That's not how it
works. Instead, we should view evil as opportunistic, passing like
an electrical current through the world and through people; or
wandering like an infection that takes up residence in individuals or cultures from time to time."[45] As a wandering electrical
current passing through all of us—transcending the distinctions
between good and evil people, the conflicts between good and evil

societies, and the clashes between good and evil civilizations—
evil depends on numerous conscious and unconscious, social and
historical connections that almost always keep humans mutually
entailed in one another's lives. Nineteenth-century theologian
Friedrich Schleiermacher thus said of "original sin" that it is "not
something that pertains severally to each individual and exists in
relation to him by himself, but in each the work of all, and in
all the work of each; and only in this complete character can it
be properly and fully understood."[46] Evil "spreads," then, not by
reason of its own discrete power, but by opportunely exploiting
social relations that often present themselves as goods.

This mutual entrenchment of evil with good should have special relevance when we consider the actions of the powerful today.
The leaders of the Bush administration, and especially Bush himself, deploy rhetoric in terms of the opposition and struggle of
good with evil. This book focuses on the attacks of 9/11, but
other examples abound: a bombing in Iraq; a destroyed nightclub
in Indonesia; a school massacre in Russia; or the other terrorist incidents worldwide that have increased in number since the
invasions of Afghanistan and Iraq. Bush's explanation is routine:
"This is a battle of good versus evil. *They* hate *our* freedom." This
understanding of evil, along with an inability to admit mistakes
on important matters (or even smaller ones), has been analyzed
by ethicist Peter Singer in the context of many policy issues: stem
cell research, government funding of religious organizations,
making war, deliberating about abortion, same-sex marriage,
combating AIDS and poverty.[47]

Though he lays claim to a mantle of Christianity and is declared
by the Christian Right as its leader, George W. Bush's mantra-
like invocation of the good on his side, with God on his side, is a
betrayal of one of the deepest roots of Christian faith in the New
Testament, that is, a capacity for self-critique: for an open-eyed
sense of limit and fault and, at least, recognition of one's potential
for error and for violating even our own most cherished standards
and ideals. No wonder that citizens, with or without religious
backgrounds, asked Bush in the 2004 presidential debates, "Can
you name mistakes you've made?" (He barely suggested there were

some but refused to reveal any.) Most dangerous of all, perhaps, is Bush's seeming inability to question his own Christian faith. Bush has repeatedly been touted by the Christian Right as "chosen by God for this hour in our nation," and he accepts those accolades seemingly with no sense of ambiguity. He takes it in full accord with his own sense of divine calling, to which he attributed even his decision to run for the presidency. It is hard to be self-critical of one's faith and policies if one is believed to be in one's position as a result of divine election. Howard Fineman summed it up in *Newsweek*: faith "helps Bush pick a course and not look back."[48] That confidence of faith is to run rough-shod over Christian faith, to ignore the point that evil works in the allegedly evil and the allegedly good. Bush's sense of divine election, mixed with an inability to question his policy and faith, is a dangerous combination in a leader, especially in the highly nationalistic period of post-9/11 American romanticism, which I examine in later chapters.[49] Now, however, let us turn to a second but related point about how evil works.

EVIL AS PRIVATION

If evil is no mere opposite of the good, it is understandable that it distorts by taking an acknowledged good, leaving its trappings in place (as so much disguise and dress), and twisting the good toward destructive ends. Again, to cite a well-known saying of Jesus, we know the point well: "Beware of false prophets, who come to you in sheep's clothing but inwardly are ravenous wolves" (Matt 7:15). This is no simple matter of disguising the evil by covering it with some pleasing or innocent-looking costume. The relation of evil to the good is more complex than that, and comes thus even more stealthily upon us. Here is where Augustine's point is helpful. Evil is "a privation of the good"; it is *of* the good but then takes something away from it. Augustine's perspective here is, again, that evil is an operation performed upon the good, that it is intrinsically bound up with some good.

Tillich also picked up on this notion of evil twisting the good in his concept of "the demonic." He did not mean a realm of demons working on a supernatural plane and intervening in humans' lives. Instead, "the demonic" was his term for structures of evil in public life that had both broad public appeal (seemingly good) but which twisted the good to work widespread destruction. In this sense, Nazism's rise to power would be demonic, coming into being by a complex set of actions that distorted certain goods in public life.[50] Just one of Tillich's passages on the demonic displays his complex approach to the entanglement of good and evil: "The demonry of the state, church, and economics is visible when the holiness of these social forms, their right to sacrifices, is misused destructively—wherewith as a result the self-destruction, namely the shaking of the belief in their holiness, is connected."[51] The crucial point here is that Christian theologies that reflect New Testament understandings of evil stress that evil often comes as a distortion of the good, that it comes distorting *publicly appealing structural forces that pose as good.*

We may at times wonder amid experiences of evil: Is evil only a matter of distorting or twisting the good? If we approach it that way, can we do justice to the full trauma of our times? When we ponder the ruinous policies of our nation in Iraq (not just the numbers of *our* dead but the thousands of innocent Iraqi citizens lost while generals like Tommy Franks say, "you know we don't do body counts"[52]), when we meditate on the gutting of international law by the present Bush regime, when we remember administrators like Defense Secretary Donald Rumsfeld and White House lawyers discussing the torture of captured enemies in terms of how much damage to internal organs really constitutes a violation of their human rights, when a leader like Ariel Sharon in Israel can take credit for leaving the Gaza strip while razing homes and leaving precious little but rubble and ruin for more Palestinian families, or, when, on the other side, we face up to the brutal ways of Saddam Hussein, of al-Qaeda, of suicide bombers, and more—considering all this, it is tempting to say that evil is just counter to the good. It seems simply awful, "implacably hateful," as Elshtain repeats, so there is no need to try to understand it. To many, trying to "understand" seems like toleration of evildoers. I understand this reaction. Evil has such destructive force against everything we hold dear that it does seem mere anti-good power. But I would nevertheless argue that for evil destruction to become comprehensive, routine, and as widely destructive as it often has been and is today, there must be the insinuation of evil *into* the good, its posing as good, and its distorting *of* the good. Hence, my procedure here is to treat evil as a distortion of the good. If we wish to stop evil, we must analyze how it is insinuated into the good. When we identify a force or forces as evil, we do well to ask, "What good is being distorted?"

The idea that evil comes as distortion of the good provides a helpful way of examining the rise of militant terrorism and Islamism. What good is distorted by al-Qaeda? Few in the American public, however, are ready to grapple with that kind of question. Understanding that lack of readiness comes from analyzing how the goods of U.S. culture and society have been distorted, bearing their own "evil" propensities. It is precisely those distortions that we will examine in chapters 2 and 3.

It may be objected that the harsh criticisms of the Bush regime that I have already made, and my book's subsequent criticisms of American romanticism and contractual liberalism, yield but a "reverse Manichaeism," a dualism of the left that takes aim at evil just as vigorously as do those deploying the reigning rhetoric of evil I lament in this chapter. This objection, though, represents a misunderstanding of my project. When I decry the romanticism and nationalism of Pax Americana, or the liberalism of our time that is corrupted by a managerial and corporatist liberalism, I am not simply marking those off as evil in themselves, in terms of the dualism of good and evil functioning in today's political rhetoric. In contrast, these forces and structures that I criticize are presented throughout the book as distortions of the good, as deceptive twists given to ways of being in the world that are in themselves good (e.g., our need to belong to place and group, our need to expect future growth and flourishing). The distortions I critique are derailments of human aspiration by destructive cultural habits and traditions that we must learn to resist.

This respect for the mutually coinherent relation of evil with the good is the major feature that keeps my criticisms from being

a mere reverse Manichaeism. Moreover, while I support movements for the removal of leaders of the Bush regime, even believing
with Amnesty International that criminal investigations and pro-
ceedings against officials high in the Bush administration should
be begun for human rights violations and war crimes,[53] this is
a much more measured response than the Bush regime's Manichaean reflex to launch preemptive military attacks (often against
international will and law) on those it deems "the enemy."

In addition, as illustrated by my book's concluding proposals
for a restored sense of American belonging and for a renewed (if
radicalized) liberalism, the book seeks to untwist, as it were, and
to correct for distortion the deep running social, personal, and
political vitalities that have erupted so destructively in our time,
especially after 9/11. It is this 9/11 moment to which we now
turn.

2

THE 9/11 MOMENT

The assault on the World Trade Center was
unpardonable, but it is important not to lose
perspective, especially a historical one. . . . The scale
and consequence of the September 11 attack are massive
indeed, but this is not the worst act of mass terrorism
in U.S. history, as some U.S. media are wont to claim.
The over 3,000 lives lost are irreplaceable, but one
must not forget that the atomic raids on Hiroshima and
Nagasaki killed 210,000 people, most of them civilians,
most perishing instantaneously.

—WALDEN BELLO, *DILEMMAS OF DOMINATION*

Most people would say that September 11, 2001, was a
momentous day in their lives. If time did not quite stand still,
it felt as if it had been made full, laden with heavy meaning. The
minutes and hours of that morning would become so full that the
time took on a new quality. We might call it a *kairos* moment,
a segment of our lives within ordinary, chronological time but
within which both crisis and opportunity, crossroads and decision, seemed suddenly to loom before us. Many people speak of
the day in those terms.

What happened? What was the 9/11 moment? In what ways do
U.S. residents still live under its spell? This chapter only begins
to answer these questions. To understand more fully "what happened on 9/11," the chapters on American romanticism (chapter
3) and on contractual liberalism (chapter 4) will also be crucial.

Many if not most U.S. citizens would counter this chapter's opening quotation from Walden Bello, a professor of sociology and public administration at the University of the Philippines, with two responses. First, 9/11's dead should be differentiated from Hiroshima's and Nagasaki's dead on the grounds that these nuclear attacks took place during an already declared war and thus do not deserve Bello's claim that the United States' atomic raids in Japan were acts of "mass terrorism." Second, U.S. citizens might agree that those raids, in the nation's past, were monumentally terrorizing to Japanese civilians but still hold that 9/11 is unique because it occurred on U.S. soil. Those making this type of response might be challenged to remember the four thousand dead on U.S. soil from a forced march in 1838 and 1839 during which over 25 percent of the Cherokee nation died.[1] Other critics have reminded U.S. citizens of "the other 9/11," September 11, 1973, when the U.S. supported the overthrow of a democratically elected government in Chile, clearing the way for military dictator Augusto Pinochet, whose regime sacrificed tens of thousands of Chileans.[2] But then the debate continues, with consideration of the unique surprise, shock, and spectacle of 9/11 in New York and Washington, DC in 2001. So the day continues to loom large and unique for many U.S. citizens, no matter how many examples of other events might be cited to place in various kinds of analogy to the 2001 event.

So what is the nature of the event citizens of the U.S. and the world refer to as 9/11? What kind of moment was it? And what is meant when referring to "post-9/11 USA"? In this chapter I begin a response to these questions by distinguishing the event as both a historic moment and a mythic moment. The basic claim of this chapter is that 9/11 *as a historic moment,* having some unique traits and a special historical impact, does not adequately account for the significance and resonance it had at the time and still commands today. There are too many other events in history that have at least some meaningful similarities to 9/11. It is 9/11 as a symbolic event, as *a mythic moment,* especially for many U.S. citizens' mythic understanding of their nation, that accounts for the uniqueness of 9/11.

THE HISTORIC MOMENT

For the United States, the events of September 11, 2001, and the post-9/11 developments are full of historical drama. In *The 9/11 Commission Report,* the summary of the drama is stark: "On September 11, the nation suffered the largest loss of life—2,973— on its soil as a result of hostile attack in its history."[3] This description is usually accompanied by countless stories and mini-histories involving persons, families, workers. Citizens of the U.S. and of other nations too, near and far from New York and Washington, DC, found their comings and goings full of new meaning.

A few days after the attacks I walked in New York's Union Square with my daughter, who was soon to be living in a New York University dormitory nearby. Union Square had become a public site for families and friends of the dead, grieving their losses or seeking the missing by posting photos, laments, poems, prayers. They also scrawled their epithets of rage. The unity of work and remembrance, forged amid unfolding trauma, reminded me of the families of the disappeared I had seen in offices in Latin America. These, too, were public sites with walls of hastily posted family photos, pinned-up poems, prayers, and sorrow-songs for their missing. Those offices were in places like Guatemala, Honduras, Colombia, Argentina, Peru, Chile, and elsewhere, but they had displayed the same resilience of humanity amid massive sorrow that I saw in New York City as it grieved its dead and missing. In spite of all the criticisms I direct toward the U.S. government's response to 9/11, I shared, in my own ways, in the grief and rage of citizens under attack that day, and both the grief and rage are understandable and warranted.

Beyond the sorrows of the day, which victims' families above all carry with them to this day, there were many other aspects of 9/11 as a historic moment. By "historic" I am referring to the plethora of recountable events, some dramatic in nature, some less so, but all of which make up describable (and often debatable) activities and processes surrounding 9/11. Among them are such matters as the effects on New York City's urban architecture and air quality, and new challenges posed to urban living. Victims' families had to be compensated, and debates raged about which funds should be used (federal, state, city) to bring relief, and how large the grants should be. National and international air travel was immediately suspended, and, when it was restored, passengers would experience a whole new set of travel rituals and security precautions.

The nation's economy trembled, symbolized by the closing of financial markets for a five- to six-day period. New budget priorities emerged featuring altered funding patterns as enormous sums went to surveillance and military operations in the United States. War—advocated by many and protested by many—became a ubiquitous public concern as the Bush regime moved abroad militarily (first in Afghanistan and later in Iraq), allegedly to retaliate for the 9/11 attacks and to counter the threat of terrorism in general.

Also in the immediate post-9/11 environment, new powers were allocated to the federal government, and it exercised them quickly. In the first weeks after the attacks, new domestic security policies tightened surveillance, and, with the controversial USA PATRIOT Act of October 25, 2001, civil liberties were curtailed.[4] In the same month, the executive branch went to Congress to press for massive tax cuts for some of the most powerful corporate supporters of executive office holders.[5]

At the same time, even while many citizens were ready to trust the federal government with these new powers, many harbored and voiced profound suspicions. Understandably, the suspicions emerged because 9/11 was a massive drama and it takes time for a public mind to assess it. But the 9/11 drama became all the more baffling when the U.S. President's office delayed its support for investigations. Then, once they had begun, the Bush administration made known its reluctance to cooperate at various points along the way. And even after the investigations, unanswered questions persisted. The unresolved questions generate melodramatic conspiracies across Internet culture, making many a reflective citizen understandably cautious about both executives' and legislators' accounts of the 9/11 events. Just a few of the troubling unanswered questions are these: Why does the Bush administration continue to cultivate its close ties to the ruling Saudi regime?

Why were some twenty-eight pages of *The 9/11 Commission Report* whited out? Why have more than two dozen former U.S. intelligence and security officers criticized the serious omissions in the *Report*?[6] There are numerous other such questions that have undermined the confidence of many in U.S. leaders' accounts of 9/11.[7]

Taken together, all of these factors only begin to scratch the surface of discussions of the historical events relating to 9/11 and of the debates about it. It is not the purpose of this book to press for clarity on these difficult matters. Rather, we need to interpret 9/11 in terms of what we know about its impact on U.S. public mythology. Here we draw closer to understanding the interplay of religion and politics in the post-9/11 USA.

THE MYTHIC MOMENT

September 11, 2001, was momentous within the paradigm of most U.S. residents' understanding of the myth of America. We might begin to understand this first by turning to developments across the recent decades leading up to 9/11. Particularly in the period of Ronald Reagan's presidency (1980–1988) there was a revival of what historians of the United States have termed "American exceptionalism."[8] The basic idea here is that the United States views and promotes itself as the exceptional place, the scene where a people and government are caught up in divinely inspired, historical unfolding.

American exceptionalism is deeply rooted in the discourse of early American preachers and political founders. Puritan founder and governor of the Massachusetts Bay Colony, John Winthrop (1588–1649), dreamed of the new experiment of governance in North America as being like "a City upon a hill." In the 1980s discourse of President Reagan, the U.S. beckoned to all humanity as a "shining city." Sensibilities like these had powered many U.S. citizens' visions of manifest destiny, which animated the U.S. history of expansion and imperial vision—first across the North American mainland and then, from 1898 on, further West out into and across the Pacific.

However one evaluates Reagan's policies, he possessed rhetorical skills to affirm and reaffirm this U.S. national mythology in the recent period. In the 1980s, Reagan used the myth of America to promote visions of the nation as a wondrous exception in the world order. He drew upon that myth especially when promoting a technological dream of military prowess that technocrats, then and now, find hard to create: the Strategic Defense Initiative (SDI). The SDI sought to build an impenetrable shield over the country, a "roof" over the United States, to protect it. Thus there would also be protection for what Reagan termed "the divine plan" at work in this nation between two oceans, where people "had a special love of freedom" and where they were coming together to create "something new in the history of mankind."[9] As historian G. Simon Harak has pointed out, this language is fully consistent with key features of American civil religion. In that religion, America is seen as "the virgin land" protected by two oceans, innocent of the corruptions of the Old World, and blessed with a new mission for the world.[10] During his presidency, Reagan directed his listeners to focus on a distinctive threat to their nation, a threat that could come from the skies, from nuclear missiles. This could defile the sacred land and rupture the nation's invulnerable sanctity, its sacred soil. Well before 9/11, then, Reagan was enlivening citizen concern that foreigners had the ability to attack America from the skies and pollute our Eden.

The enduring mythic understanding of the Eden-like nation, protected between its oceans and chosen for a divine destiny, together with Reagan's revival of new senses of the nation as frontier, constructed the mythic backdrop against which the uniqueness of the 9/11 moment can be discerned. It was "morning in America," as Reagan's winning campaign slogan had it. Although his vice-president and successor, George H. W. Bush, couldn't quite match Reagan's rhetorical gifts in order to preserve the full force of the myth, his "New World Order" and the claims of his 1991 State of the Union address to have overcome the Vietnam syndrome with a Desert Storm victory in the Gulf War were interpreted and promoted to the citizenry as a renewal of America. Throughout the roaring 1990s, Bill Clinton and his advisors spoke of the coming twenty-first century as U.S. leaders had in previous times, as "the American century."

The morning in America on September 11, 2001, ruptured this mythic view. It was not destroyed; indeed the myth would surge with new strength. But the damage was real. As a mythic moment, 9/11 was felt as a violation of the sanctuary between oceans. The weapons used that day, hijacked commercial airliners, were not the nuclear missiles of Reagan's nightmare. Still, the attacks from the skies on 9/11 exploded with an impact that was momentous for Americans because of the way Reagan and so many before him spun the myth of a protected and divinely sanctioned America.

The sense of a protected, Edenic nation was further shaken for those steeped in the myth because the targets of the attack were the most visible public symbols of the nation's military and economic strength—the Pentagon and World Trade Center. The U.S. society's strength is buttressed within the world order—militarily, economically, and politically—by planners and organizations identified with those sites. When the towers came down in a repeatedly televised global spectacle of disintegration, the myth of U.S. invulnerability and of its divinely blessed national vocation was publicly and dramatically ruptured.

The fact that these symbolic sites were targeted also differentiates 9/11 from the Pearl Harbor attack, which is often compared to 9/11. Pearl Harbor was certainly an event of shock to the U.S. populace, and it also was an occasion for mobilizing massive patriotic reflexes toward war. But two differences from 9/11 are important. First, the attack was not on the mainland itself, even if the attack on a U.S. territory in the Pacific was felt as frighteningly near. Second, and perhaps more important, the attack on Pearl Harbor's military installation could be processed by the U.S. public as an attack by one military party on another. The 9/11 attacks had a distinctive symbolic impact because they took place on the U.S. mainland, at the heart of two of its greatest cities, *and* targeted world-renowned symbols of U.S military hegemony (the Pentagon) and global economic power (the World

Trade Center). The Pentagon and World Trade Center functioned as icons of U.S. military and economic power, even if that power is in fact more dispersed and not limited to those sites. The replayed videos of the disintegrating financial towers could understandably be unnerving to people whose material being is secured by the powers associated with those icons of U.S. dominance.

This mythological or symbolic impact may seem to pale in comparison to the horrors of the physical tragedy of 9/11. No one should underestimate the enduring sting of the real loss of a loved one in the 9/11 moment, which was suffered by so many that day. But the mythic impact is important, too. Let us also not forget that myths, especially in the United States, structure a people's sense of belonging to land and space; they enliven a people's allegiance to their land. Myths charter the ways people navigate their physical, social, cultural, and political existence. Myths provide a somewhat elusive but still powerful tone and sensibility that affect one's security and sense of meaning, one's place not just in the nation but on earth and in the cosmos.[11] Mythological impact, then, is no simple opposite to physical impact. The mythic moment of 9/11 is as important to consider as its historic moment.

MYTHIC RESTORATION AND TWO STREAMS OF AMERICAN NATIONALISM

This view of 9/11—as a rupture of U.S. citizens' mythic sense of American exceptionalism—is crucial for understanding the nation's entry into the opening decades of the new century. If 9/11 damaged America's sense of invulnerability, it is equally true that this also has led to a massive drive in the U.S. to restore an Eden-like sense of invulnerability. It does not matter whether the invulnerability was in large measure an illusion or it cannot be recaptured. The loss is nonetheless felt and expressed in the many efforts of citizens to restore a sense of invulnerability. It accounts, in part, for the intense fear in U.S. citizens. The fear isn't just "of terrorists" in the sense that each U.S. citizen thinks there might soon be a bomb in his or her neighborhood, at the shopping mall. No, the substantive fear, I suggest, is a more subtle and general one. It is a more deeply registered apprehensiveness resulting from the fact that the terrorist attack removed the sense of protection under the sacred canopy of national greatness. A restorationist drive to recapture that felt greatness, mingling with the fear of future attacks, is what government can exploit, promising security in exchange for citizens' giving up their liberties.[12] This is why the Congress could roll back civil liberties through its 2001 USA PATRIOT Act and why the Bush administration sought in 2005 to extend powers of the state security apparatus even further. The 2001 Act had set expiration dates for government exercise of new invasive practices, such as the "sneak and peek" searches that involve entering private premises without a warrant and postponing notice to the citizen until after the search, if notification is made at all. The 2005 revisions sought to suspend the expiration dates for some sixteen provisions of the 2001 Act that were previously scheduled to expire in 2005.[13]

It is this restorationist drive that also accounts for the resurgence of U.S. patriotism. So strong has the post-9/11 patriotic reflex been that writers have called it "superpatriotism" or "hyperpatriotism."[14] In the two to three months after September 11, 2001, more flags were sold in the U.S. than at almost any other time in U.S. history.[15] So strong has the patriotic reflex been that freely expressed dissent has often come under profound suspicion. Media figures and citizen groups as well as politicians and government officials tend to affirm patriotic conformity more than they speak of guarding civil liberties. Even sectors of American liberal culture, which, before 9/11, cultivated a certain sophisticated aloofness from the hoopla of patriotic hyperbole and celebration, sought after 9/11 to conform to the patriotic culture, if only by being less vociferous in making criticisms. This self-monitoring can reinforce the fear and rage that after 9/11 have driven many into an ardent patriotic spirit.

Many U.S. citizens, and I count myself among them, critique and resist this new hyperpatriotism and the quashing of dissent that often comes along with it. Especially those groups in the U.S.

who have known themselves to be marginalized and oppressed by U.S. power in the past (Native, African, Latina/o, and Asian Americans; unionized workers; immigrants; and others) enter the sphere of hyperpatriotism a bit more cautiously, if at all. In 2003, only 38 percent of blacks, compared to 65 percent of whites, self-identified as "very patriotic."[16] Yet many from these groups have been so startled by the dismantling of American invulnerability in the post-9/11 milieu that they, too, now often either willingly embrace the new hyperpatriotism or feel pressured to do so.

Patriotism, though, is not nationalism. Anatol Lieven, citing one of the greatest recent historians of nationalism, Kenneth Minogue, points out that nationalism benefits from patriotism but brings a more serious order of problems. Whereas patriotism often mixes a love of one's country with commitments to fight for the revered land as it is, nationalism usually entails a program or project that aggressively pursues certain additional ideals. Nationalism has, in Lieven's words, a "certain revolutionary edge," a "messianic vision."[17] To work at this edge and pursue a messianic vision, leaders of nationalist projects usually have to appeal to the most readily available ways to maximize their citizens' energy and support. Patriotism, especially in a hyperpatriotic atmosphere fueled by fear and insecurity, is one such way. Aspiring leaders of nationalist projects will also discourage challenges to their plans by deploying force—from expropriated labor, regressive taxation, racist stereotyping, and curtailment of citizen liberties to martial law, brutal policing and paramilitary pressures, torture, and war.

As historic and mythic moment, 9/11 has created an especially aggressive nationalist project from long-standing currents of American exceptionalist national identity. Americans' exceptionalist national identity has slipped into nationalism before, in European settler communities against Native American peoples, in justifications of slavery, and especially during other times of war: notably the Mexican War, the Spanish-American War, the World Wars, and, to varying degrees, the Korean and Vietnam conflicts of the Cold War period. Again, too, the United States is not unique among the world's nations for fusing nationalist projects with messianic vision and chauvinistic aggression.[18]

Today's U.S. nationalist project, however, has some unique features. It is especially aggressive and virulent because of the dramatic nature of the 9/11 event *as a mythic moment,* enhanced by its sudden explosiveness on the U.S. mainland, and as a media spectacle that could be witnessed throughout the nation and world. Moreover, the nationalism that has emerged in U.S. government after this mythic moment possesses its unusual features because of the ways religious and secular forces are working together through a special set of alliances and cooperative strategies toward what I call a "revolutionary romanticist agenda." These unique alliances and cooperative strategies will be examined throughout the following two chapters.

It is helpful, as in Lieven's work, to view the resurgence of a virulent nationalism after 9/11 as the ascendance of one of two forms or "two souls of American nationalism" over the other.[19] Lieven doesn't state what he means by his characterization of these currents as "souls." It is more helpful to think of them as two streams that feed into and forge U.S. nationalism in different ways. Each stream brings a distinctive ethos, a special cultural tone and way of living carried by different social groups.

One stream is a more traditionalist one, drawing from the Protestant and Anglo-Saxon elements of European settler communities. Lieven terms the resulting kind of nationalism from this stream an "ethno-religious nationalism," one that typically has been more aggressive, celebrating white, manly performance along frontiers where cowboys, soldiers, and explorers prove their mettle and character, usually through conflict with nonwhite, alleged "enemy combatants" (Indians, Spaniards, Mexicans, Filipinos, Japanese, Vietnamese, Arabs, and so on). It is this stream I will examine as the specter of American political romanticism in chapter 3. It is this stream, this "soul" of American nationalism, which is now ascendant in the post-9/11 USA and gives special strength to its imperial regime.

The other stream presents itself as the more enlightened of the two forms of nationalism, its soul, or ethos, shaped by allegiance to the "American creed." It celebrates, in the nation's rhetoric, a commitment to a democratic project, to an ethos of liberalism in which liberty and equality for all is valued. Indeed, this creedal nationalism, or "civic nationalism," as Lieven calls it, has kept in check some of the worst excesses of the ethno-religious form of nationalism and has been used to some good effect by marginalized and subordinate groups to gain greater freedoms. Nevertheless, this alleged liberal ethos has been sorely constrained, usually operating under the mandates of racial, sexual, or class contracts (often hidden from mainstream public view) that severely limit the efficacy of the liberal vision. This civic nationalism will regularly put aside its enlightened commitments and compromise, making common cause with the other soul, the ethno-religious one with its more chauvinistic nationalism. It is this civic nationalism, and its disingenuous liberalism, that I will treat in chapter 4 as the specter of contractual liberalism. As we will see at that later point, ethno-religious nationalism has grown ascendant over civic nationalism, and, after 9/11, many who would champion the more liberal, civic, or credal ethos of nationalism are making common cause with it.

THE SPECTER OF AMERICAN ROMANTICISM

But the history of humanity gives us no reason to
suppose that we will ever cease to mythologize and
mystify the origin and history of our societies.

—RICHARD SLOTKIN, *GUNFIGHTER NATION*

Prophetic spirit is in struggle with both of what Anatol Lieven
termed the "two souls" of American nationalism, each pointing
to distinct but interplaying currents of nationalism, each carrying a distinctive ethos. Prophetic spirit must work to understand
the ethos of each, their origins, and how they interplay to unleash
destructive forces today.

Understanding each ethos will require our viewing them
within the powerful historical currents in U.S. history that have
made them the strong options they are, that give them a kind of
soul-power in life and politics. This book situates each nationalist
ethos within a distinctive cultural-political current of American
life.

The more traditionalist ethno-religious nationalism is animated
by the cultural-political current of American romanticism.[1] It is
the burden of this chapter to understand that romanticist current.
Civic nationalism also has its romanticist dimensions, but historically it is carried and animated more by another current, the contractual liberalism I examine in chapter 4.

As we turn to American romanticism, the carrier of ascendent
ethno-religious nationalism of the post-9/11 USA, we might now
appreciate Lieven's use of the term "soul." He displays a perhaps

unconscious cunning in using the term. It is helpful because it suggests that there is something about these nationalisms that is not merely a political configuration in the present. Rather, these nationalisms tap into often hidden recesses of peoples' historical and political living, dimensions where historical actors, movements, and social groups wrestle with pervasive questions about being. Nationalisms exploit a social ontology; they give national drama to citizens' search for meaningful existence. Their actors, movements, and groups seek to realize ways of being and manifest styles of pursuing and maintaining meaning in their lives. Nationalism, then, has a centering, animating, driving quality that, as soul, should not be seen as an immaterial quality but as a hidden, energizing dimension at work in the social, political, and material dynamics of that nationalism.

This chapter begins, therefore, with a section that links the stream of American romanticism to its soul and understands it as a way of being that I call "belonging being." The chapter's second section will suggest how this stream grew stronger as a result of the 9/11 moment. The third and fourth sections, on the Christian Right and the neoconservatives respectively, show how both religious and secular groups exploit the romanticist interest in belonging being for the present imperial politics of the United States. The final section, "A Deadly Alliance," will show how these religious and secular groups are now working together to fuel a revolutionary romanticist project.

"BELONGING BEING" AND AMERICAN ROMANTICISM

American romanticism is a current of U.S. history, culture, and politics that drinks deeply of the human species' propensities to celebrate and revere its origins. It might be better to speak of "American *political* romanticism" because romanticism is also a movement in literature and philosophy in Europe, the U.S., and elsewhere, which carries more meanings than the political and nationalist ones I explore here.[2] The current of American romanticism displays reverence for, is in thrall to, "belonging being." This is a way of being that is marked by personal or group senses of belonging to the past, to past traditions, nations, peoples, lineages. The romanticist sense of belonging is so crucial to existence that one's being is understood as a belonging to these past traditions, these origins. To use "belonging" as an adjective for "being" here can seem awkward, but it is my way of accenting how strongly this current takes senses of belonging to be, how it emphasizes the cultivation of senses of belonging, all as *a way of being and living in the world*. Humans almost everywhere are born into existence with a sense of belonging to places, times, and groups, but they do not always place a premium on that sense of belonging for living and being as does political romanticism, and the American romanticism treated in this book.

Having a particular origin and cultivating a love of those who seem to share that origin are very powerful, even if one has strong suspicions, even rage, about what that collective body has suffered or what its leaders have done to one's own group or to others. The United States' cruel policies of massacre and removal of indigenous peoples, centuries of slavery in American soil, overt and covert wars against other nation's peoples—all this can sow rage, yet without destroying a sense of belonging to, even a reverence for, origins. There often persists a strange love for one's collectivity, even among descendants of those victimized by their nation's past. Keep scratching away at the surfaces of the most hardened cynic about American patriotism and you will often find a desire to revere, to hold in some ideal or model form, a virtuous past or certain virtuous figures. Even if we radically demystify the cults of George Washington, Thomas Jefferson, or Abraham Lincoln, or those of Mark Twain, Walt Whitman, or Ralph Waldo Emerson, still, there is often some faithful remnant of heroes and heroines, some Harriet Tubman, Frederick Douglass, Lydia Maria Child, John Brown, Dolores Huerta, Michael Harrington, or Emma Goldman. A few cynics may be able to stamp out this will to mythologize the past of one's own collective origins, but rarely does the whole collective body eradicate the reverence for origins, the powerful call of belonging being that is expressed and shaped by a romanticist ethos. Richard Slotkin, the great scholar of American mythology, especially the myth of the frontier, wrote: "The history of humanity gives us no reason to suppose that we will ever cease to mythologize and mystify the origin and history of our societies."[3]

In the United States, the most recurrent expression of this belonging was American exceptionalism, the sense that I have already argued has gained new strength from the Reagan years through the 9/11 moment to today. American exceptionalism begins with a conviction that the U.S. is a unique nation with a cause that transcends its borders. This could be developed along lines of a Bible commonwealth, as did early New England settlers, invoking a righteous empire that, by the mid-nineteenth century, was described as America's "manifest destiny," willed by God for expansion and the bringing of American goods to the world.[4] In later, more secular, forms, others still spoke of the good nation, an exceptional experiment among the nations, but invoked a more secular language of "democracy and freedom." Thomas Paine (who was not a Christian), for example, wrote on the first page of his *Common Sense*: "The cause of America is in a great measure the cause of all [hu]mankind."[5]

The romancing of America occurs in both religious and secular types. The religious type closely links reverence for the nation's origins with its origin in and dependence upon God—with all the risks of heating up nationalist fervor with religious fervor and also the risks of destroying religion by reducing it to idolatry of the nation. The more secular type romances America by linking reverence for national origins with a vital force. Examples of this force, this public energy, would be senses of republican virtue, of civic spirit, of democratic propensities, or a general sense of "American Greatness," this latter being a term used especially by the neoconservative Pentagon planners that we will discuss below.[6] There is here still an exceptionalist reverence for the nation and for belonging to it but without obvious religious trappings.

Another distinction regarding American romanticism, especially important for understanding American religion and politics today, is between conservative and revolutionary types of romanticism.[7] This distinction does not parallel the first one, that is, conservative romanticists are not necessarily religious people, and revolutionary romanticists are not necessarily secularists. Instead, the conservative–revolutionary distinction is one that cuts across the religious–naturalist distinction, bringing new dynamics onto the political scene.

Conservative romanticists—whether religious or secular—revere national origins by criticizing and avoiding new systems and events in hopes of preserving elements of an idealized past. They attempt to back away from new forms of modernity, to get back to a preferred past. Conservatives strengthen romanticism's ethos with a strong preservationist agenda. Revolutionary romanticists, on the other hand, seek to revere national origins through an all-out attack on newly developed forms and systems. Revolutionaries not only idealize and revere "founding fathers," they declare various kinds of war on the modern nation insofar as it is deemed to have exceeded the vision and intentions of founders. In contrast to the moves conservative romanticists make to preserve or restore the past, revolutionary romanticists seek to roll the modern system back, to take it on, to dissolve its alleged progress, interpreting that progress as so much backsliding from revered origins. In short, both conservative and revolutionary romanticists share the goal of celebrating past national forms as ideals for the present, but they differ as to their means; the conservatives' actions are largely those of protection and preservation of past ideal forms, sometimes acting to resist changes in the present, whereas the revolutionary romanticist wages vigorous and trenchant resistance to modern structures in the present that are seen as violating the past ideals.

Romanticists can take up the more aggressive revolutionary agenda, in both religious and secular modes. In the religious mode, they might become revolutionary romanticists in their all-out resistance to the U.S. case law that has established a separation of church and state, or in their vigorous organizing to secure a judicial overturning of Roe v. Wade, because of moral or theological objections. In the secular mode, they might make war against arrangements established with other nations that have become part of modern life and international systems. In both cases, whether religious or secular, revolutionary romanticists seek to dismantle what are perceived as modern "liberal" systems and structures.

ROMANTICISM AND THE 9/11 MOMENT

The consolidating power of two noteworthy groups in the post-9/11 USA displays what has happened to American romanticism in the most recent period. These two groups enter media commentary and analysis as "the Christian Right" and "the neoconservatives." In this chapter, I interpret them as contemporary configurations of the long-running stream of American romanticism, differing from one another as religious and secular types of romanticism, respectively. Yet they are both romanticists with revolutionizing agendas.

The religious romanticists—in the form of the Christian Right, whose very leader held the White House in the hour of 9/11's rupture of American exceptionalism—seek to bring back notions of the United States of America not just as an exceptional nation but also as what historian Martin Marty has analyzed as "righteous empire."[8] Thus the tendencies toward Christian theocracy in U.S. government are very strong throughout many departments of U.S. governance today. Bush has touted the Bible as a regulatory guidebook for organizations receiving government funding through his faith-based initiatives. Theocrats—self-identified as such—roam the White House and even meet with National Security Council officials.[9] President Bush opens his cabinet meetings with prayer, which can become disconcerting for Christians and non-Christians who do not share his prayer tradition.[10]

The secular, or naturalist, romanticists, represented today by the "neocons," or "vulcans"[11] (doing their work primarily through the think tanks of the American Enterprise Institute and the Project for a New American Century and elsewhere) urge trust not so much in religious empowerment but in unrivaled military power to shore up "American greatness." These neoconservatives were also high up in U.S. government in the hour of 9/11's rupturing impact, having already worked throughout the 1990s to create a more robust U.S. military hegemony. The neocons are now strategically cooperating with the Christian Right to achieve a revolutionary agenda that rolls back long-standing modern commitments of U.S. government, both at home and abroad. Their successes to date are due in large part to their post-9/11 power to exploit citizens' romanticist sense of belonging being. They thus often gain tolerance, if not outright support, from the wider sectors of the U.S. public. The revolution is underway—whether the theocratic dreaming and planning of the religious romanticists of the Christian Right, or the military-imperial dreaming and planning of the typically secular neoconservatives—and it is well described in Paul Krugman's discussion of the "revolutionary power" at work today. He writes in hope of a "great revulsion" among the populace against the power play of both groups. Alas though, as he says, quoting a passage from Henry Kissinger's published doctoral dissertation, *A World Restored,* "Those who warn against the danger in time are considered alarmists; those who counsel adaptation to circumstance are considered balanced and sane."[12] To understand the danger better, we must look closely at both the Christian Right and the neoconservatives.

THE CHRISTIAN RIGHT AS RELIGIOUS REVOLUTIONARY ROMANTICISTS

The term "Christian Right" can be misleading. It is often taken to refer to a group of individuals in U.S. party politics who embrace Christian faith and vote for those having moral values consistent with that faith. The Christian Right is better understood as a powerful romanticist movement in the revolutionary mode that has new powers in federal government and has created well-funded structures that affect federal policy. It is the purpose of this section to describe some of the key aspects of this religious movement's power today.

In contrast to analysis of the Christian Right as movement, both advocates and critics of the Christian Right show a tendency to fixate on George W. Bush's personal piety. Advocates for Bush's piety, as in their 2004 video release *George W. Bush: Faith in the White House*, situate the Billy Graham—converted Bush within a line of god-fearing presidents who, as they emphasize, were not afraid to blur the lines between church and state.[13] Similarly, those less impressed by Bush's piety, such as the narrators in the 1999 PBS video *The Jesus Factor*, still focus the debate around the individual faith of George W. Bush.[14]

Focusing on Bush's individual piety is understandable in that today Bush, while in the office of president, is proclaimed as "the leader of the Christian Right" even by those who self-identify as members of that group. As Kevin Phillips has pointed out, this is in contrast to previous decades when a leader of the Christian Right (Jerry Falwell or Pat Robertson, for example) had the mantle of leadership and then entered into various kinds of relationship with a president (Reagan and Bush Sr., for example) who curried favor with the American religious right but did not explicitly count himself as one of their number. But Bush Jr. is now himself that leader, acknowledged as such by Gary Bauer, for example, the evangelical leader and one-time candidate for president against Bush in the 2000 Republican primaries.[15]

All the focus on Bush, however, can obscure the extent of the Christian Right's influence as an organized, dynamic force today. This force lies in the way it purveys a long tradition of religious romanticism, giving divine sanction to American exceptionalism and thereby providing added public strength to nationalism, especially of the more chauvinistic varieties. The video, *George W. Bush: Faith in the White House,* even invokes the phrase "American exceptionalism" as a tradition that U.S. citizens, and especially Christians, should affirm. The Christian Right also brings great fervor to its organizing within U.S. governance. Today, the Christian Right carries its religious romanticism into U.S. government in two ways: by spreading a ritualized religious ethos in the corridors of U.S. power and by constituting powerful new structures at strategic points in U.S. governing institutions.

So pervasive and extensive is this religious romanticist ethos that multiple books are addressing it. I can only summarize briefly what is involved. Here, I depend heavily on the rich investigative journalism and documentation of Esther Kaplan in *With God on Their Side* (2004).

A Ritualized, Religious Ethos

Presidents and government officials in the United States have always brought their pious practices and poses into their workplace. Numerous officials in the Bush regime, however, have placed into U.S. governance a more routinized practice of Christian faith.

The Bible as a Guidebook. The Bible, in the form used by Protestant Christians, has received a special sanction in the ritual life of Bush's governing practice. Bush himself reads biblical passages within evangelical devotional literature. Using the Bible or other collection of sacred writings is not a problem. But when he holds up the Bible, as he did once, referring to it as a "guidebook" for a faith-based group receiving federal government funds, he crosses a line and presents personal religious preference as a federally funded perspective in the government of a multireligious society.

Weekly Bible Studies. According to David Frum, an orthodox Jew who was a speechwriter in the early days of the Bush regime, weekly White House Bible studies (attended by more than half the staff) were "if not compulsory, not quite non-compulsory either" and so "disconcerting to a non-Christian like me."[16]

Revival Meetings. Bible studies were also frequent at Attorney General John Ashcroft's office. *The Washington Post* reports lunch-time revival meetings "making the front hall sound more like the foyer of a Pentecostal storefront church."[17]

Religious Symbols. Routinely issued government documents are given religious symbols. The Department of Labor's Faith-Based and Community Initiatives office features, in full-color, a print of a bush in flames with the caption: "Not everyone has a burning bush to tell them their life's calling."[18] This may be a harmless deployment of a symbol from religious literature (the story of Moses and the burning bush in the Hebrew scriptures). Taken, however, with the other markers of Christian ritual ethos and along with the structures I discuss below, the practice easily can slant government toward a pro-Christian perspective.

Religious Language. Bush's speeches often embed terms and phrases that seem to broadcast only the usual American civil religion, but actually "narrowcast" more specific religious meanings to his evangelical faithful, such as when he spoke of the nation's "wonder-working power" (a phrase from a Christian hymn about the power of "the precious blood of the lamb"), or when he ends his speeches with his own distinctive line, "May God *continue to* bless America."

Symbolic Physical Representation. At key presidential speeches, such as the State of the Union addresses, religious leaders are often seated near to the first lady and to others of the president's family.

Meetings with Leaders. On policy drives across the country, campaigning for support in funding his Iraq assault and occupation or for his privatization program for Social Security, Bush regularly links up with leaders of Christian Right groups (who also, by the way, had held a ritual, laying hands on him to commission him after he announced that God had called him to seek the presidency).[19]

Social Gatherings. Bush also provides special social gatherings for devotees of the Christian Right, usually associated with official events in which they have a stake. According to journalist Esther Kaplan, members of the evangelical groups Focus on the Family and the Family Research Council were proud to be at a private gathering with Bush before he officially signed the Partial Birth Abortion bill. In fact they rode *with* Bush in a motorcade to the signing ceremony.[20]

Again, these markers of Christian ritualized ethos in governance may be seen as no more problematic than any of the other markers of the ways past presidents have brought distinctive features from their own different personal backgrounds and convictions into executive branch culture. It is important to see, though, that when a Christian ritualized ethos is marked at as many points as it is in the Bush regime, it lets loose into government culture one of the most powerful traits of religious symbols: their active power, in anthropologist Clifford Geertz's language, "to establish powerful, pervasive and long-lasting moods and motivations" in people.[21] Those who bring powerful convictions into governing policy need to check to make sure that those of alternative religious persuasion are not placed in a subordinate position by such moods and motivations established in the cultural system. Clearly, something like that subordination is evident in the quote by David Frum in the "Weekly Bible Studies" item above.

The moods and motivations of Christian ritualized ethos become even more problematic when they lead a president to hold up scriptures sacred in his own tradition as a "guidebook" for a federally funded program. Perhaps especially problematic is that so very few of the "faith-based" social programs that the Bush administration has approved for funding are non-Christian. It is difficult to gain access to files showing all groups that have received government funding, but Kaplan reports, "in examining hundreds of grants from the faith-based offices at Labor and at Health and Human Services, in such areas as job training, work placement, child support, and abstinence education, I found that—with the exception of a few interfaith groups—*every single religious organization that had won a grant was Christian.*"[22] When a presidential regime's Christian ritual ethos accompanies output that is skewed in this manner, a society diverse with many religions and secular vocations has a right and a duty to be suspicious that governance is not being exercised fairly, that it is failing to respect the diversity of religious expression that is expected in a democracy.

THE CHRISTIAN RIGHT'S STRUCTURAL POWER

More significant than the religious ritualized ethos are the polit-ical powers of governance under Christian Right influence and control. Again, the Christian Right has a power of influence well beyond its percentage of U.S. population because of particular political alliances it has made.

Kaplan reports that the Christian Right has an "ornate and sta-ble infrastructure of hundreds of national and local membership organizations." Many of these have budgets running to the $100 million level, with radio and television industries reaching mil-lions. These build networks among tens of thousands of Chris-tian churches and parachurch groups, and such networks include heavily endowed think tanks, professional agencies, and political action committees.[23]

According to Kaplan, many of these organizations first came into being after the U.S. Supreme Court abortion decision of Roe v. Wade in 1973, thus producing influential groups with leaders who are prominent throughout right-wing religious circles: Judy Brown of the American Life League, James Dobson of Focus on the Family, Phyllis Schlafly of the Eagle Forum, Beverly LaHaye from Concerned Women for America. These groups and more like them campaigned for Bush in the 2000 election and then helped drive Bush's policy to cut U.S. funding for any interna-tional women's groups that counsel women abroad about even the possibility of having an abortion. The effect of this policy is to sup-port restrictive abortion laws that have helped force some 20 mil-lion illegal procedures worldwide every year, causing more than 700,000 deaths annually, according to the World Health Organi-zation's data.[24] These Christian Right groups have also organized preferential support for those judiciary appointments by Bush of judges who consider Roe v. Wade not as a complex decision about a complex matter, but simply as "the worst abomination."[25]

Regarding judiciary appointments and the appointments of the Attorney General, the Christian Right has been especially active. When Bush, in his first term, offered his own conservative choice for U.S. Attorney General, Christian evangelicals orga-

nized through the American Conservative Union behind John
Ashcroft, a still more conservative figure who opposed abortion
even in cases of rape and incest. Ashcroft, once appointed, later
promised to dismantle former Attorney General Janet Reno's task
force for stopping deadly attacks against abortion providers.[26] In
spring 2005, Republican Senate Majority Leader Bill Frist of Ten-
nessee appeared and spoke in support of a major telecast, organized by the Christian Right's Family Research Council, that
portrayed the Democrats' filibustering against a few of President
Bush's numerous judicial appointments as "judicial tyranny over
people of faith."[27]

In Bush's first term, John Ashcroft had brought into the highest judiciary office of the land a strong version of American
exceptionalism and also certain theocratic aims. In a speech at
Bob Jones University, Greenville, South Carolina, he intoned:
"Unique among nations, America recognized the source of our
character as being godly and eternal, not being civic and temporal. . . . We have no king but Jesus."[28]

The Christian Right is also uniquely connected to Bush's policies regarding Israel in the Middle East through its support of the
Likkud Party, a stalwart bastion of Israeli nationalism. "Christian
Zionist" movements in the U.S. have grown to record numbers,
powered by their belief that Israel's full return and settlement
of the biblical lands is a necessary condition for Jesus' return,
the second coming. The Left Behind series, a set of novels about
Christ's second coming, the rapture of Christians, and the slaugh-
ter of the heathen, are now reported to be the best-selling novels
for adults in the U.S. Indeed, the series is "by a long stretch the
most successful series in the history of American print fiction."[29]

Kaplan estimates that Christian supporters of Israel possess
even greater influence over U.S. policy on Israel than the American Israel Public Affairs Committee (AIPAC) or other Jewish
lobbies, having special access to leaders like Republican Majority
Leader Tom DeLay. Hundreds of thousands of Christian donors
and supporters, mobilizing millions of dollars through networks
of as many as 25,000 churches, work through such organizations
as Americans for a Safe Israel, Christians' Israel Public Action

Campaign, Stand for Israel, the Friends of Israel Gospel Ministry, Christian Friends of Israel, Christians United for Israel, and the International Fellowship of Christians and Jews. Members of the Christian Zionist and theocratic "Apostolic Congress" have actually been present at U.S. security briefings discussing policy with White House personnel such as Elliott Abrams, a Bush senior Middle East liaison officer.[30] Respected journalist John Cooley, with over forty years of reporting and investigation in Middle East nations, has documented well how relations among the U.S. government, Israel, and Christian Zionists in the U.S. helped shape the disastrous policy of war against Iraq as finally implemented in March 2003.[31]

Numerous posts throughout the government—in the Department of Labor, in Health and Human Services, in federal family planning programs, the Presidential Drugs Advisory Committee, the Centers for Disease Control's National Center for Environmental Health—in all these areas and others, the Christian Right has managed appointments to key positions from which religious romanticist agendas are to be pursued.

As a final example of this structural presence of the Christian Right, I note the very important Council for National Policy, which nurtures connections between the Christian Right and powerful conservatives in corporate culture.[32] This council includes not only representatives of the major Christian Right organizations mentioned above, but also conservative corporate donors; former cabinet members from the Reagan administration; the president of the Heritage Foundation; Grover Norquist, president of an anti-tax group; Brent Bozell of the Media Research Council; and many other powerful figures connected to academic think tanks, corporate wealth, and military industry.[33] Why is this problematic? It is because the networking among these elements concerns governance crucial to the economic and political life of all our nation's residents, and yet it takes place under largely Christian auspices and, generally, outside of public purview. As I will make clear when discussing contractual liberalism, this link to corporate worlds is crucial for understanding the enormous, disproportionate power and organization of the Christian Right.

Its influence is so far-reaching, in part, precisely because of these
ties to U.S. corporate power.

It is important to pause over this point for emphasis. The Christian Right with its moral values did not, by itself, put Bush and
his agenda in the White House, as is often implied. White evangelicals are routinely pointed to as the base for Bush's agenda.
As stressed at the outset of this book, not all who self-identify as
evangelicals support the agenda of the Christian Right. Moreover,
as a voting block, white evangelicals and the Christian Rightists
among them are not the most formidable source of Bush's Republican victories. "White evangelicals" constitute only 23.1 percent
of the U.S. population. Even though they made up 40 percent of
Bush's popular vote in the 2000 elections and 36 percent in the
2004 elections,[34] sociologists have shown that in presidential elections their voting block has affected only 1.6 percentage points of
the Republican total votes gained.[35] In close elections that can
be determinative. Nevertheless, the Republican Party is far more
dependent on another block of voters, the affluent 20 percent of
U.S. voters with incomes over $75,000 a year. This voting block of
affluent citizens reliably affects nearly 4 percentage points nation-
wide in presidential elections on behalf of Republican presidents,
thus having twice the electoral power than white evangelicals for
the Republicans. Moreover, the affluent voting block can use its
wealth and connections to shape electoral processes in other ways
that are not available to the less affluent among white evangelical
and other groups. Thus, if the Christian Right is to have deter-
mining power on elections and federal governance, it will have to
work in tandem with, or maintain connections to, that wealthy
sector. One of the ways it does that is through structures like the
Council for National Policy. This underscores a point made from
the beginning of this book: the power of the Bush and Christian
Right agenda does not rest only in itself but in the ways it has organized in relation to other powerful sectors, to the neoconservative movement I discuss in the next section, and to the powers of
contractual liberalism discussed in chapter 4.

It should be apparent now, also, that the Christian Right's
influence is not to be presented as a secretive cabal, as in so much

conspiracy theory. We are faced not with a cabal, but with a well-organized social movement, one at work throughout federal and state government with a recently intensified religious ritual ethos and newly organized structures for federal governance. As Kaplan has observed, even if Bush and the Christian Right's government appointees were turned out of office today, the work already done has been so vast, in both government and society, that the impact will remain large for the foreseeable future.[36]

We must turn now to the secular revolutionaries, the neoconservatives, who have entered into alliance with the Christian Right.

THE NEOCONSERVATIVES
AS SECULAR REVOLUTIONARY ROMANTICISTS

In almost any polity, there are persons and groups ready to use nationalist ideology and the obedience nationalism fosters in citizens to implement their own agendas. The revolutionary romanticism of the Christian Right, in a religious mode, is but one way nationalism has been strengthened and exploited in the post-9/11 moment. There is another active mode in this moment, working revolutionary romanticism in a more secular vein. Today's bearers of this more secular revolutionary romanticism are those who have been dubbed, often by themselves, "the neoconservatives."

The term "neoconservative," shortened today as "neocon," has its origin in American socialist Michael Harrington's "act of dissociation" from one-time socialist and old liberal comrades in the 1970s. When the latter groups threw their weight behind the Vietnam War and expressed their revulsion for the antiwar left culture, Harrington refused to see them even as a venerable "right wing of the left." As Gary Dorrien relates in the second of his two fine books on neoconservatism, according to Harrington, they belonged to "the left wing of the right."[37] According to Dorrien, the committed socialist Harrington labeled as "neoconservative" such figures as Arnold Beichman, Sidney Hook, Emmanuel Muravchik, Arch Puddington, John Roche, and Max Shactman.[38]

Old liberals gone conservative, or "neoconservative," were persons such as Daniel Bell, Nathan Glazer, Henry "Scoop" Jackson, Max Kampelman, Jeanne Kirkpatrick, Irving Kristol (the first figure among those on this list to accept the label and work out the notion of neoconservative[39]), Daniel Patrick Moynihan, Ben Wattenberg, and others.

After some grumbling, these figures accommodated themselves to the Republican Party, largely during Ronald Reagan's administration, beginning in 1980. What differentiated them from the long-running traditions of American conservatism? After all, their vision of "American greatness" (a term affirmed often by neocon Irving Kristol) and their insistence that U.S. regimes should pursue that greatness, was animated, in large part, by the sense of American exceptionalism that conservatives had long revered. In this sense, both the neocons and the so-called paleoconservatives, or traditional conservatives, drank deeply from similar cultural and political streams of American romanticism. The difference is that the neoconservatives pursue a more revolutionary romanticism, without nostalgia or restorationism, and often without the isolationism that marks the more traditional American conservatism. According to Dorrien, even as they found a home in the American Right, they brought with them "a more dramatic idea of politics, especially in foreign policy, to promote, expand and sustain America's global dominance."[40] Central to the neocons' more dramatic ideal was their aim to maintain a unipolar order, with the United States being the unrivaled superpower.

It should be stressed here that this goal of the neoconservative American right, this revolutionary romanticism, is not limited to the Republican Party. Even if Republican regimes, from Ronald Reagan to George W. Bush have given it their most virulent and aggressive expression, Democrats also promote the neocon agenda. This is signaled by Democratic Senator Henry "Scoop" Jackson's popularity with the early neocon movement. Moreover, the neocons' unipolar world began to be developed by Pentagon officials during the Clinton administration as "full-spectrum dominance,"[41] a policy that aimed to assure that the next century would remain an "American century," the latter phrase use by Clinton's first Secretary of State, Warren Chris-topher, as he handed over the reigns of the State Department to Madeleine Albright. Albright herself would refer to America as "the indispensable nation." (U.S. officials' tendency to claim the whole century as "American" goes back at least to the administra-tion of Franklin Delano Roosevelt.) Democratic Party politicians and foreign policy planners, even if they are less visible than the Republican neoconservatives, still frequently give strength to the neocon "persuasion," as it is termed by the oft-acknowledged neo-con godfather, Irving Kristol. William Safire even greeted John Kerry during the 2004 presidential campaign as "the newest neo-con," because of his hawkish military tactics and grand strategy.[42]

What surfaces in contemporary politics today, then, is not just a strong Republican Party but a resurgent revolutionary roman-ticism powered by Republican regimes, with significant support from Democrats and from other citizens and officials of many different persuasions. Their shared revolutionary romanticism thrives on the newly intensified American exceptionalism and nationalism that have pervaded U.S. politics and culture since the 9/11 moment.

As noted above, the neocons in the second Bush administra-tion were strategically positioned in the 9/11 moment. When fear, shock, and hyperpatriotism flooded American culture and public sensibilities after 9/11, the neocons already had an impressive infrastructure in place. Not only were they politi-cally unified, possessing key administrative posts in the Bush administration, they also had assumed control over leading conservative publications like *The National Review, Commentary,* and *The American Spectator,* which are serviced by think tanks ("patriotic monasteries," as military historian Chalmers John-son dubbed them[43]) such as the American Enterprise Institute, the Hoover Institution, the Manhattan Institute, the Center for Security Policy, and others.[44]

Perhaps the neocons' most important instrument throughout the 1990s was its paragovernment organization, the Project for a New American Century (PNAC). Founded in 1997 by Irving Kristol's son, Harvard-educated William Kristol, it was funded by the Lynde Bradley Foundation as was the American Enterprise Institute, from which the Bradley Foundation rented its office space.[45] Its goal was to promote the exceptionalist aim of American greatness, but according to its influential 2000 publication, *Rebuilding America's Defenses,* it aimed at a more vigorous strategy for outfitting the U.S. military's unipolar drive toward U.S. dominance. This was a call for the fulfillment of a vision to expand the U.S. military, which had emerged from Paul Wolfowitz and other Pentagon officials in the first Bush administration.[46]

The PNAC enabled the neoconservatives to hone their policy and lobby for it through publications and in open letters disseminated during the Clinton years. Many neoconservatives assumed positions in the new Bush regime of 2001. Of eighteen PNAC members who signed a January 1998 open letter to Clinton advocating that "removing Saddam Hussein . . . needs to become the aim of American foreign policy," eleven of them went on to important positions under Bush (Richard Armitage, Donald Rumsfeld, Elliott Abrams, John Bolton, Paula Dobriansky, Zalmay Khalizad, Richard Perle, Peter W. Rodman, William Schneider Jr., Robert B. Zoellick, and Paul Wolfowitz, whom Bush appointed in 2005 as World Bank president.). Dorrien gives copious examples of how the neocons' unipolarist visionaries of American greatness pervaded the Bush administration of 2001: "unipolarist appointments went all the way down."[47]

In *Rebuilding America's Defenses,* the PNAC admitted that their prescriptions might not find political support without the rallying power of some "new Pearl Harbor."[48] They got that rallying power from the 9/11 moment, bringing as it did an abundance of hyperpatriotism that swelled support for renewed military build-up and for near perpetual "war against terror."

The neocons, notably Rumsfeld and Wolfowitz, wanted to go into Iraq immediately after 9/11 but settled for the more justifiable target at the time, al-Qaeda in the Taliban regime's Afghanistan. Soon, though, the new, more militarized Bush brought his public rhetoric as president into much closer relation to the long-standing neocon agenda, especially with its goal of removing Hussein's regime in Iraq.[49] Dorrien reports that Bush ordered a secret war plan against Iraq "less than two months after the U.S. attacked Afghanistan," in December 2001.[50] In their book, *America Unbound,* Brookings Institution senior fellow Ivo Daalder and a Council on Foreign Relations director and vice-president, James M. Lindsay, quoted President Bush as saying, "Fuck Saddam, we're taking him out," in March 2002. Bush reportedly uttered this to Condoleeza Rice "as he poked his head in her White House corner office as she was meeting with three senators to discuss what to do about Iraq."[51] Not only was this four months after the Afghanistan campaign began, it was a full year before the March 2003 U.S. invasion of Iraq. Reports from the "Downing Street memos," communiqués summarizing British officials' views that the U.S. planned as early as July 2002 to attack Iraq, also suggest the long-standing intent to invade Iraq. The evidence is fairly strong that Bush, by mid-2002, shared the neocons' resolve to move militarily against Hussein's Iraq no matter what Hussein did or did not do in response to whatever the UN mandated during the months of 2002 and early 2003. So strong was the neocon intention of the Bush regime to invade Iraq, despite lack of proof of Iraq's complicity in 9/11 or of its holding weapons of mass destruction, that Hussein probably could not have done anything to avoid the U.S. assault.

A DEADLY ALLIANCE?

It is not my purpose in this book to lay out a thoroughgoing critique of the Bush regime's policy in Iraq. Its duplicity and failure have cogently been laid out by others.[52] More important is why that critique has so little bearing on national policy and why the U.S. public remains supportive or tolerant of the policies of war and violations of civil liberties. We gain some understanding of the resilience of the neocon power play if we recall that its public persuasiveness rides the romanticist current of American exceptionalism. It is a revolutionary romanticism that differs from more conservative romanticisms in that it leads with an ebullient, aggressive nationalism, one that the neocons see attractively modeled by Teddy Roosevelt and especially by Ronald Reagan.[53] Both of those former presidents galvanized American exceptionalism by tapping into some of the most powerful images of the U.S. myth of the frontier, that boundary region where American national identity was often forged by romanticizing soldierly virtue displayed against usually nonwhite "enemy combatants."[54] In fact, PNAC Deputy Director Thomas Donnelly explicitly deploys the U.S. frontier paradigm for his vision of the U.S. military as "the global cavalry" that is "patrolling the perimeter of the Pax Americana." Further, "like the cavalry of the Old West," whose military presence anchored settler's expansion into indigenous nations' lands and Mexican territories, this global force today works through overseas bases to form what Donnelly advocates as a necessary "system of frontier stockades."[55] Not all romanticisms drawing strength from American exceptionalism display such a bold throwback to Old West mythology. But the neocon revolutionary romanticists revel in it.

Neoconservatives succeed in all this because largely secular officials have strategically allied their revolutionary romanticism with the revolutionary agenda of religious romanticists, the U.S. Christian Right. In turn, the Christian Right has been ready to baptize the neocons' aggressive, unipolar militarism with its vision of a righteous kingdom. Theocratic impulses working in tandem with militarist impulses yield an especially aggressive nationalism.

At times this alliance is quite fragile, as when some Christian Right figures foreground their anti-Semitic Christian conversionism, which might alienate those intellectuals and pundits among the neocons who are Jewish.[56] Apparently, the neocons' commitment to American greatness dovetails sufficiently with the Christian Right's American exceptionalist notion of manifest destiny that any ill-feeling over religious contentiousness can be overlooked. Leo Strauss, one of the theorists informing several key neocon Bush appointees, in fact, encouraged wise rulers to deploy strong doses of state-oriented religion to unite the polis, even if the virtuous leaders of that polis do not themselves believe in that religion.[57]

Many analysts today have sounded an alarm about the prevalence of right-wing movements in the turn-of-the-century USA. They have highlighted, across numerous studies, the roles of the Christian Right and neoconservatives. Both are, indeed, problematic, and not just singly, but in their post-9/11 alliance. They undermine democratic aspirations because of their unabashed advocacy of concentrated power. The Christian Right boldly devalues the importance of a pluralism of viewpoints, grows more belligerent when it sees itself under attack for its conservative views, resists processes of checks and balances, responds to dissenting government persons with retaliatory audits,[58] all largely driven by a fervor to protect its understanding of biblical values. At the same time, the neoconservatives boldly advocate their unipolarist strategies to secure full-spectrum dominance of the world order, launching military projects unilaterally, reneging on international treaties and agreements, even rationalizing, as we have seen, a practice of torture against decades of cooperative discussions codified into international law.

Both the Christian Right and the neoconservatives share a fervor and political will to constrict power to one group and to one nation. Such a constriction of power is a fundamentally anti-democratic practice. Democracy at its best is about openness to challenge, deliberation, and often compromise within a wide variety of dissenting voices and opinions. George W. Bush's most natural language regarding his own power is telling. He told author Bob Woodward: "I'm the commander—see, I don't need to explain—I do not need to explain why I say things. That's the interesting thing about being president. Maybe somebody needs to explain to me why they say something, but I don't feel like I owe anybody an explanation."[59]

The mix of authoritarian nationalism with a messianic project is, as Anatol Lieven points out, often rooted in compensations that certain groups or classes in a nation seek as a kind of salve for shame and humiliation. He argues that this is one important part of what we see in the rise to power and support for today's religious and secular romanticism. The "poisoned" nourishment of radical nationalism is defeat and especially humiliation.[60] The

9/11 moment in itself was not so much a blow to citizen pride in American exceptionalism, but a trigger for a resurgence of those groups whose romanticist desire for return to an idealized past aims to redress group feelings of defeat and embattlement. Lieven identifies "four distinct but overlapping elements of the American national tradition which mix shame and humiliation with support for radical nationalism: the original, 'core' White Anglo-Saxon and Scots Irish populations of the British colonies in North America; the specific historical culture and experience of the White South; the cultural world of fundamentalist Protestantism; and the particular memories, fears and hatreds of some American ethnic groups and lobbies."[61]

Lieven's entire work on these groups, in relation to U.S. nationalism, needs to be examined carefully because it illuminates the different ways that each of these groups is at work in today's U.S. nationalism. Michael Lind has related Bush's Texas background to these traditions of Scots Irish groups, especially in the oligarchy of the White South.[62] The argument, again, is not that today's virulent nationalism and aggressive imperial unilateralism are only due to a humiliation suffered on 9/11, but that groups already steeped in cultures of felt defeat and embattlement have harnessed the fear and patriotism of the post-9/11 moment for their ends. One hears often from spokespersons of the Christian Right that "modernists and secularists" are out to "destroy our faith" or are "attacking us." Voices claiming to speak from a more progressive or modernist commitment often fan the flames of such humiliation with attitudes of class disdain for those uncomfortable with or alienated from a fast-paced, customs-challenging modernity.[63] In the post-9/11 moment, powers are at work through both religious and secular romanticism to vigorously re-implant an idealized past in resistance to a modernity they see as threatening.

What is particularly disturbing is that the religious and secular romanticists in the post-9/11 USA have entered into a more cooperative alliance, one that yokes religious and political agendas in ways that may sound a death knell for the functioning of democracy in U.S. domestic governance and international policy. Indeed, the quite real deaths of thousands of Iraqi civilians as a result of the religious right's and neocon's war and occupation of Iraq since 2003 are striking testimonies to the deadliness of this alliance. Does it also spell death for the American democratic republic? Anatol Lieven, writing in *America Right or Wrong,* suspects that with just one more serious attack on U.S. soil, the kind of ethno-religious nationalism virulently at work in the Bush regime will not be containable by the more "enlightened" civic nationalism.[64] In *The Sorrows of Empire,* military historian Chalmers Johnson writes that he fears it is already too late, that the American republic's decline has already begun, that "Nemesis, the goddess of retribution and vengeance, the punisher of pride and hubris, waits impatiently for her meeting with us."[65]

My argument here is that if U.S. citizens are going to challenge the deadly alliance between the Christian Right and the neoconservatives, we need to understand both of them as American romanticist movements that are exploiting, in a revolutionary way, the American exceptionalism that feeds off citizens' sense of belonging to our nation. Citizens' overwhelming need for belonging has been abundant since 9/11, becoming a veritable blinding force that enables those seeking to usurp power for their own religious and political agendas to act in exploitative ways.

If this deadly alliance is to be resisted, it will be because U.S. residents find another way to speak to this need for "belonging being." Is there another American romance that can be delineated, one that better serves democratic projects and guards against usurpations of power that deal death internationally and nationally? Without finding that better way of belonging being, the star of empire that some proclaim as the nation's glory will become an ever more vainglorious star, a nemesis to others and to itself.

4

THE SPECTER OF CONTRACTUAL LIBERALISM

Where is Grotius' magisterial On Natural Law and the Wrongness of the Conquest of the Indies, *Locke's stirring* Letter Concerning the Treatment of the Indians, *Kant's moving* On the Personhood of Negroes, *Mill's famous condemning* Implications of Utilitarianism for English Colonialism, *Karl Marx and Friedrich Engels' outraged* Political Economy of Slavery?

—CHARLES MILLS, *THE RACIAL CONTRACT*

The other soul of American nationalism, to recall Anatol Lieven's formulation, is the ethos that gives rise to a creedal, or civic, nationalism. This is the kind of nationalism with which the spinners of American public rhetoric usually lead for presenting U.S. government in its most positive light. Lieven and others see this nationalism as constraining the excesses of the other ethno-religious form, even though they admit that civic nationalism has weakened in late-twentieth- and twenty-first-century contexts. I argue in this chapter that not only has it weakened, but it now often makes common cause, as it has in the past, with the ethno-religious nationalism.

The key elements of this civic nationalism, which constitute for Lieven an "American creed," are "faith in liberty, constitutionalism, the law, democracy, individualism and cultural political egalitarianism."[1] Lieven and others have argued that these elements have been regular themes throughout U.S. history, even if often infrequently realized. They are usually seen as stemming from the Enlightenment's idea of emancipating reason, long-nurtured in English political systems and theories, born again through an "American Enlightenment," which gave rise to the U.S. national experiment in democracy in the Constitutional Convention of the late eighteenth century.

It is important to stress that civic nationalism does not move through history as a set of principles. As with ethno-religious nationalism, we must avoid speaking of "the American creed" or of U.S. civic nationalism in only the formalist terms of "American values" and "fundamental truths," as do, for one example, the "just war against terror" scholars who have used those "truths" to justify U.S. actions abroad. No, the creed and its principles are carried by historical currents of social practices that both enable and constrain them. The current that is most relevant to American civic nationalism is "contractual liberalism." As with American romanticism, this cultural-political current gives expression to, and then distorts, a necessary dimension of human being. Contractual liberalism is another specter, one specter that has haunted and still haunts our political lives with the threats of empire. Contractual liberalism, while touting progress and liberal largesse and while celebrating its allegiance to the American creed, has also subverted that creed. As we will also see, especially in post-9/11 USA, the specter of contractual liberalism exacerbates the specter of American romanticism at work today.

"EXPECTANT BEING"
AND CONTRACTUAL LIBERALISM

The historical current of contractual liberalism, which carries American civic nationalism, is rooted in a sense of "expectant being." U.S. residents, like many others, not only are thrown into existence with a reverence for origins, with a sense of "belonging being," they also lean forward into a future, and so manifest "expectant being," anticipating growth, progress, and improvement. The roots of civic nationalism and of the contractual liberalism I discuss in this chapter lie in ways of being that practice a drive toward the new, the future. These roots have traits, dynamics, and problems that are distinct from those marked by belonging being; nevertheless, expectant being and belonging being are usually co-present in groups and persons. Belonging being and expectant being almost always grow together, even though they may be differently related to each other in different historical periods and national contexts, and even though in this chapter the major discussion will focus largely on expectant being.

Especially if economic well-being or political freedom is severely curtailed, the human propensity to anticipate and seek improvement, to demand change, is strong. This is often true even of romanticists' revering of origins, though their tilt to the past is stronger. The animating vigor of expectant being is in tension with romanticism since it reveres the dynamics that belong to the future more: change and growth. This often can mean embracing the dissolution of past political and religious forms, subjecting them to critique and development. The need to belong *and* the need to expect are closely bound with one another, and so American romanticism and contractual liberalism will also be in complex interplay. Nevertheless, it is important to distinguish them because groups in history tend to organize themselves according to one more than the other. Moreover, to understand how the two unite in a particular period it is necessary to see them first as distinctive cultural-political groups.

To live in expectation of the new is an animating ethos often referred to as "liberalism." The meaning of this term has changed from context to context, even over the course of U.S. history, and many different meanings have been attached to it.[2] "Liberalism" is far from being "the expression of a single project," as Jeffrey Stout has cautioned.[3] Nevertheless, it can be taken as naming a cultural-political current of history that carries with it several ideologies claiming defense of individual liberty as a guiding value, especially in systems of government. Further, individual rights, especially for those in particular subordinated groups, came to be advocated after the Enlightenment period, making those rights a key feature of a "modern liberal period" in the West. It is probably best to say that liberalism consists of several traditions. I am suggesting that it be viewed as a way of being, a way of expectant being, that infuses an ethos into many dimensions of life.

Liberalism's ethos, then, influences more than just theories of government. It also has a distinctive effect on social life generally, on knowledge, as well as on political theory. Insofar as liberalism pervades social life, it propels personal lifestyles and moralities, group life and organizational dynamics toward new forms, often dissolving traditional forms and social bonds. As to knowledge, a liberalism of thought at least claims to, and often does, celebrate an ever critical rationality and deliberation, raising further questions, pressing new inquiries and types of reflection toward fresh insights of reasoning, even new alternative views of what reasoning is. This lively rationality also nurtures discovery that is at the heart of innovation and technology. Politically, liberalism's commitments are usually summed up by referring to principles of extending and expanding liberty and freedom, especially for individuals, with at least some claims that hierarchies and alienating authorities need to be responsible to the rights of the people. In all these areas—social life, knowledge, and politics—the future is looked to as revelatory, enlightening, for a present reaching toward some better time.

The tragedy and moral failure of expectant being is that the liberalism it assumes and claims to foster has almost always been contractual. By "contractual" I do not mean that this liberalism involves explicitly made business agreements, contracts in a narrow commercial sense. Nor do I refer to the contract that "social contract" theorists (Thomas Hobbes, John Locke, Jean-Jacques Rousseau, John Rawls) often delineate and advocate as necessary for the social functioning of liberal society and the rules to which it needs to agree.[4] I mean, rather, that liberalism, even when speaking about liberty and freedom and while claiming to maximize those values, has always been practiced in a restricted manner—restricted to a select body of people. Liberalism in the West and its virtues of freedom have been, one might say, "under contract"—that is, subject to formal or informal agreements that limit the field of those deemed worthy of freedom. Western liberalism, for example, was long restricted to predominantly European political bodies that drew resources from peoples of Latin American, Africa, and Asia, while denying them participation in the benefits of European growth. Colonialism and neocolonialism, as privileging Europe in this way, are examples of contractual liberalism, of liberalism organized in a way that is restrictive and hence subversive of its own ideals. Political scientist Ira Katznelson notes that the better analysts of liberalism acknowledge "that all liberal regimes are based on foundations of state violence and coercion," and that this cannot be ignored even when we admit the virtues of liberal social discourse, which often champions liberty and freedom.

The modern European world system tended to root liberal discourses of freedom and equality (as developed mainly by Hobbes, Locke, Rousseau, and Immanuel Kant) in its assumption that its civil society was working out a social contract to which all humanity had agreed. This purportedly explained Europeans' own rise out of a state of nature and how all other peoples might do the same so they could be assimilated as equals in a global civil society led, of course, by European civilization.

The social contract theory has come under numerous criticisms. As philosopher Charles Mills points out in *The Racial Contract,* Europeans never really imagined themselves as having been in the same state of nature in which they saw various non-Europeans to be embedded.[5] The social contract they devised and advocated as an ideal for agreements and for the founding of liberal society was just that, an ideal made available for a few and denied to others. Nor did they really believe that "the requisite character" for this ideal contract was sufficiently abundant in such as "Europe's women, non-Christians, the unpropertied, and virtually all of the world's population with dark skins."[6] Mills gives numerous examples of how liberalism's social contract theorists championed a rhetoric of freedom for all while believing only in a freedom for some. This limited liberalism is what I refer to as contractual liberalism. A decade before *The Racial Contract,* Carole Pateman, in *The Sexual Contract,* similarly demonstrated that Western liberalism's freedom discourses actually harbored a "hidden, unjust male covenant upon which the ostensibly gender-neutral social contract actually rests."[7] In fact, she claims that liberalism "always generates political rights in the form of relations of domination and subordination."[8]

Like Mills's work, however, and unlike Pateman's, this book will not give up completely on liberalism because, though fundamentally limited contractually, it often remains an expression of expectant being and thus cannot be simply opposed. To be challenged, it must be critically engaged. Thus the prophetic spirit I propose below will be a revolutionary form of expectant being, one that radicalizes liberalism, perhaps beyond what is traditionally recognized as liberalism. Liberalism will continue to distort and co-opt expectant being just as romanticism distorts and co-opts belonging being, unless some alternative mode, some revolutionary form of expectant being, is historically available. In this chapter, the essential point is that the cultural-political current of liberalism is severely limited. The modern liberal system is built on a contractual set of agreements that hobble an authentic, or full, liberalism. The modern liberal system was, and to a certain extent is, a modern "colonial world system" functioning not on the basis of a social contract for the freedom of all but on the basis of racial and sexual contracts (often national, colonial, and imperial, too) that maintain a distinction between the governing and the governed, the entitled and the exploited—groups of persons set apart from one another as the worthy and the unworthy.[9] The brutalities of slavery and genocide of indigenous peoples and others, therefore, could dwell alongside the liberal visions of Hobbes, Locke, Kant, and others, and alongside much-celebrated scientists like Francis Bacon.[10]

When colonial leaders in North America were invoking European liberal traditions against England's colonizing ways, they were also exercising contractual liberalism themselves. The colonies' own liberal enlightenment remained a liberalism subject to racial, class, and sexual contracts—a liberalism largely restricted in the early U.S. to white men who owned property and extending later to men who did not own property, but still not to any indigenous people or to women, and surely not to slaves from Africa.

The drive to explore and assimilate the new, so central to liberal society, also produced a European knowledge of measurement and surveying that enabled colonizing Europeans to lay down a grid on the North American lands that spurred Europeans' proprietary interests in controlling it and displacing Native peoples who took a different measure of the land. The constricted, contractual character of liberal society is especially evident in the restrictions by class, race, and gender that accompanied this enterprise of measuring and surveying North America.[11] George Washington embodied both the measuring, scientific mind and the brutal politics of contractual liberalism; before he served as president of the new "liberal" Constitutional Republic, he had been a surveyor and also was known as "town destroyer" of the Seneca.[12]

Even today, when many claim for U.S. liberal society an impressive progress that now "includes" those previously excluded from its earlier forms, the exclusionary and contractual restrictions on liberalism are still much in evidence. *The Racial Contract* and *The Sexual Contract,* as well as numerous studies of continuing structural racism and gender injustice, give evidence that liberalism's promise of progress remains severely curtailed.[13]

Moreover, from the beginning of the U.S. Constitution, economic egalitarianism has clearly *not* been a part of the American creed, and hence, to many, today's talk of a political economy that calls itself "liberal" can seem a cruel joke. The statistics on the economic limits to the American dream are familiar: among industrialized nations, the United States has often reported the fastest shrinking, smallest, most volatile "middle class."[14] The Government Budget Office says that the income gap in the United States is the "widest in 75 years."[15] Income levels and tax breaks for the upper 1 percent of income-earning families have been increasing at least since the 1980s, throughout the regimes of Reagan, Bush Sr., Clinton, and Bush Jr.[16] Domestic business and corporate cultures have not been the great multicultural sites for ending racism that they have often been touted as being. Abroad, the global "free market," while bringing temporary benefits here and there, has hardly been characterized by freedoms for all the parties involved, as U.S. and European agricultural subsidies and tariff restrictions illustrate. As revealed in the ongoing laments and organizing efforts of poorer nations (such as Brazil, India, and the other developing nations that have formed the collective "Group of 22"), economic power is not equal among the world's nations.[17]

What is occurring here is continued subversion of that human propensity for advancement, the drives and desires for the new, for expectant being—which would maximize and balance liberty, equality, and rights—by the restrictive powers of contractual liberalism. In this discernment of the power and tendency of contractual liberalism to subvert liberalism lies the seed for a full flowering of more extensive criticisms of capitalism. I do not offer here a fully developed criticism of Western state capitalism, but I can indicate the nature of the critique that is implied here.

In my critique of capitalism, I keep the attention more on an ethos pervading most capitalist cultures and systems, one that harnesses expectant being, distorts it, advocates ideals of liberal society but then robs it of its promise by accommodating to a series of hidden, and sometimes not so hidden, contracts. Part of Karl Marx's genius was exposing the hidden contract in liberal political economy, challenging its talk about the fairness of a market's exchange of commodities and its confidence in a pre-established harmony of all things. His analyses sought to break free from being in thrall to the world of commodities being exchanged (a state of "fetishism") and to examine "the social character of the labor that produces them."[18] In my terms, he laid bare a functioning "contract" that imposed and presumed an alienation and exploitation of workers who produce those commodities. Feminist critics have given still greater complexity to economic critiques of capitalism, showing how it often also exploits women's reproductive labor.[19] Analysts of European and American white racism have noted how crucial were the racial constructs and contracts in the capitalist systems of the modern colonial world system and how colonial capitalist structures worked untold suffering on global peoples of color.[20] Critics of unexamined heterosexuality have noted how sexual relationships built around an assumed and compulsory heterosexuality often create competition that contributes to the exploitative character of capitalism.[21] All these criticisms need to be developed, tested, and made stronger in order to resist the destructive dynamics of capitalist formations.[22] Taken together, these all can yield a critique of capitalism that is more subtle and comprehensive than many of the quick, blanket rejections of all market dynamics or features of capitalist systems.

In this book, the major concern is to understand and expose a pervasive ethos that attends most capitalism—that of a liberalism that is birthed by human expectant being but then develops in accord with contracts that distort and destroy human expectation. The prophetic spirit that will emerge in this book does not simply position itself against capitalism, but instead it engages, resists, challenges, and transforms the ethos of liberalism that powers so many capitalist systems.

It is important that we now make a distinction within contractual liberalism. It is not a homogeneous category, coming as it does in many forms, all of which I cannot acknowledge here. We must note, however, a difference between two major groups. First are the "corporate liberal profiteers," who give themselves and their efforts to an unbridled pursuit of profit, unmindful or uncaring about the contractual and restricting nature of their liberalism. These groups see no problem with the class hierarchy in the United States[23] or with a global market economy that, as economist William Tabb convincingly shows, is intentionally kept under the control of the powerful G7 nations.[24] Second are the "corporate cosmopolitan liberals," who have made at least some effort to correct for contractual restrictions. This latter group is more reticent about allying with the militant romantic nationalism of the U.S. and its servicing of today's runaway turbocapitalism. Corporate cosmopolitan liberalism, the gentler of the two liberalisms we might say, can be symbolized by the side of Bill Gates that opposes the Bush administration's repeal of the estate tax. It might also be symbolized by figures, like George Soros, who have criticized Bush's romanticist ideology and corporate policy and who have given substantial funds to Bush's political opponents.

These figures of corporate cosmopolitan liberalism certainly make up a small group, but they do signal the presence of an investor class with a more self-critical relation to capitalist systems—a group that genuinely seeks to bend corporate culture, on some occasions, to the needs of those shut out or exploited by it. They at least give lip service and, at times, make a real effort not to exploit American romanticism for profit. They seek, at times, to nurture a more international solidarity, sometimes anchored in a loyalty to the globe's natural ecology.[25] They will at least voice a need to break with the sexual, racial, and other contracts that subvert liberal society. Perhaps corporate cosmopolitan liberalism is best represented not by the likes of Gates and Soros, but more by corporate officials and leaders of developing nations who guide their countries into the global market and challenge the economic power that G7 nations maintain over developing regions. These leaders often find it necessary to contest both the economic contract that favors richer nations and the racial contract favoring the predominantly white overclasses of European countries and the United States. The Millennium Project of the United Nations, which according to economist Jeffrey Sachs offers powerful countries a new and profound opportunity to redress the suffering of poorer countries,[26] has targeted the sexual contract by seeking to redress women's higher rates of impoverishment, but so far remains relatively silent about the racial contract.[27]

CONTRACTUAL LIBERALISM
AND THE 9/11 MOVEMENT

By September 11, 2001, the failure to produce genuine change toward a liberalism free of restricting contracts had arguably *already* produced a real crisis of liberalism in the United States. Especially after the fall of the Soviet Union and Eastern European socialist states in 1991, pressures grew in the U.S. to demand utilization of wealth in new ways, away from the arms-race spending of the Cold War and toward promoting economic justice at home. Thus talk of "the peace dividend" flourished in the United

States. This made the agents of contractual liberalism tremble in the face of potential social and economic reorganization. In such a context, corporatist liberals are often ready to view national and international crises as emergency conditions that would postpone any such reorganization. Thus contractual liberals, for all their differences with origin-revering romanticists, will quite readily make common cause with pre-liberal, even anti-liberal, romanticism when and if that common cause seems necessary for maintaining the restrictions (by class, race, or other categories) that undergird contractual liberalism. This means that, in spite of liberals' claimed commitment to a cosmopolitan ethos and to the liberal international virtues of the global order, many of them stand quite ready to use and allow nationalisms, especially U.S. nationalism, to have its day in order to prevent such economic reorganization.

This has happened often. U.S. businessmen sought war with Spain in 1898, for example, in part to defend economic interests and advances amid the pressure of labor disenchantment, growing populist movements, and surplus capital. They thus accommodated to the jingoist patriotism and resurgent American romanticism of that period.[28] As another example, economic managers in 1930s Germany helped deliver power to the National Socialists (the Nazis) in part because holders of wealth trembled in the face of the genuine social reorganization that was needed and being called for by powerful protest movements and a system in crisis.[29] This does not mean that the compromise with war and nationalism is only worked by the corporate classes; quite to the contrary, populist nationalisms spreading throughout all sectors of social strata also play crucial roles. But when the managerial elite of corporatist classes decide to fund and empower leaders who play to those nationalisms, the possibilities for barbarism increase. There is a tendency, in other words, for contractual liberalism, especially during crisis, to strike an alliance with forms of romantic nationalism to protect existing economic orders whose disparities of wealth make them vulnerable to critique, reform, or toppling.

In the regime of George W. Bush, especially after 9/11, this tendency has found a most willing host. Bush's regime is well-suited for welcoming contractual liberalism and for incorporating the revolutionary romanticisms (both religious and nationalist) that I discussed in the previous chapter. With this point we begin to see better why the current political situation is so dangerous. We have a regime of power forming in our midst in which the president of the most powerful nation in the world can deploy Christian rhetoric that expresses and galvanizes more than just the support of revolutionary romanticists. Also, as a son still expressing interests of a wealthy dynasty, he is attractive to some of the most powerful people in the money-making corporate classes.[30] This is his real base, not the romanticists, religious or secular. The wealthy, the "haves and the have mores," as Bush himself referred to them when addressing them at a banquet, are, as he himself *also* noted, his "base."[31] On behalf of this base, the Republicans in the White House and the House of Representatives, just weeks after 9/11 brazenly sought to cut taxes on the largest corporations, purportedly to keep the economy stimulated under crisis. As is well known, Bush went on to roll back taxes on the upper 1 percent of income earners in the country, and even began the process to end the estate tax. All this has been most welcome by agents of contractual liberalism on Wall Street. In fact, the *Washington Post* reported that the holders of wealth on Wall Street are so grateful that contributions were dumped into the coffers of the 2004 Bush campaign at unprecedented levels, surpassing all past Republican fund-raising.[32]

In the confluence of these forces within the regime of George W. Bush, we begin to see the way turbulent currents are swirling in the post-9/11 moment. The present turbulence is not new in U.S. history, but the movement of currents is at such a pace that it is often hard for viewers, and any countercultural actors, to identify and resist them.

I concluded chapter 3 by noting the deadly alliance being forged in these times between religious romanticists and secular ones, not toward conservative ends but toward revolutionary ones. The alliance there was *within* American romanticism, featuring religious and secular movements working together for a reinvigorated American nationalism, with the Christian Right often pushing a theocratic agenda, neoconservatives a unipolar-ist agenda, all to promote a Pax Americana. Together, these two romanticisms have strengthened the ethno-religious, chauvinistic nationalism of U.S. history.

Now, from the perspective of contractual liberalism, another alliance is revealed—this time *between* contractual liberalism and romanticism. This is an alliance between the two cultural-political currents that carry the two "souls" of American national-ism. In other words, the revolutionary romanticism of the American Christian Right and of the American neocon, unipolar militarists is now being strongly funded and supported by the wealthy strata of U.S. society that have been threatened by the post-9/11 instability. The threat came in the form of economic instability in the wake of 9/11 and in the form of economic disparities that had been building across the 1990s even before 9/11. Contractual liberals, using the hidden contracts of class and race (and others as well), are funding and supporting romanticist politicians and struc-tures. They are also committed to extracting new wealth from the military and surveillance technology that nationalist endeav-ors require.[33] This means that flawed, restricted liberalism is now suspending its liberal and innovative instincts in order to exploit the instincts that fuel American romanticism. The deadly alliance within American romanticism is a dangerous one in itself, but when that internally allied romanticism is additionally supported by the wealthy white overclass of contractual liberalism, the risks are even greater. Increasingly, then, U.S. society is subordinate to modern systems that are not just marked by a limited liberalism, but also by an anti-liberal practice and policy.

TODAY'S ANTI-LIBERAL MODERNISM

Contractual liberalism, as I have defined it, leads with its rhetoric of liberty and equality for all individuals and its commitment to this rhetoric is allegedly enshrined in the American creed. When allying itself with revolutionary romanticists, however, its already severely limited liberalism easily slips into an outright anti-liberalism, or what I will here refer to as "anti-liberal modernism."

Anti-liberal modernism, again, not a new phenomena, poses today a most potent threat, emerging from the contractual liberalism that U.S public life long has accommodated. What defines anti-liberal modernism is a further decay of liberalism's project in modernity; liberalism's drive toward the new, its expression of expectant being, now yields a kind of modernity that makes no pretense of liberalism (curtailing support for values of liberty, equality, tolerance, and individual rights). The new and the expected tend to be limited to the technological creativity that elites fund and develop so as to create an ever more efficient apparatus of governance and social control. There is modern technology, bureaucracy, and order, but these are distinguished neither by being shared nor by seeking a wider dissemination of goods among U.S. or global residents. Instead, it is a modernism of efficiency. Little pretense of liberalism, even in rhetoric, needs to be made. An anti-liberal spirit is pervasive, and ethno-religious, chauvinistic nationalism comes to predominate. The rhetoric of American civic nationalism is nearly eclipsed. As Franz J. Hinkelammert has noted, Western modernity has often made recourse to "efficiency" over a practice of defending peoples' rights, especially when dealing with colonized and subordinated groups.[34] The anti-liberal cult of efficiency, a disastrous and sinister undertow of Western modernity, has grown stronger as new waves of patriotism and fear break over the nation's peoples in post-9/11 USA.[35]

The neoconservatives are crucial to transforming contractual liberalism into anti-liberal modernism. In the previous chapter, I noted their romanticism, their revering of what they term "American Greatness," which, though largely secular, still accommodates symbol systems, especially from the Christian Right, that promote American "manifest destiny." But the neocons also have had access to the cultures and resources of contractual liberalism. Neocons decry liberal rhetoric as "soft" and "wrongheaded" (this is their "anti-liberal" temper), but nevertheless they still value the modernizing apparatus of governance that liberal society's knowledge programs have generated: the technologies of military and criminal justice systems, and the surveillance and judiciary processes. The neocons work not only the romanticist terrain of American Greatness but also the corporatist worlds of contractual liberalism. They are, therefore, in this historical moment, crucial protagonists of both specters of empire—American romanticism and contractual liberalism. Their spectral threat is especially evident in their anti-liberal predilections.

Neocons especially display their anti-liberal modernism in the ways they have imbibed and developed important features of a criticism of liberalism by a major intellectual, Leo Strauss. To understand the anti-liberal modernism of our times, we need to examine the way key Straussian notions have achieved resonance in policies propounded by today's neocons in the Bush regime.

Strauss taught politics to many students at several universities but most influentially at the University of Chicago through the 1950s and 1960s until his death in 1973. It is quite striking how many key officials in today's U.S. national government have been influenced by him and seek to enact his ideas. Strauss's ideas "have provided a generation of American scholars and writers with their conceptions of themselves and of their country."[36] The *New York Times* termed him "the godfather of the Republican party's 1994 Contract with America." Similarly, *Time* wrote that, "perhaps one of the most influential men in American politics is the late Leo Strauss, the German émigré political philosopher."[37] Distinguished historian Gordon S. Wood described Straussians as the "prominent conservatives in present-day American politics," and Straussians often describe themselves as "the most powerful conservative intellectual force in the academy."[38]

To be sure—and I emphasize this—the rise to power of the neocons, the agenda of the Bush regime, and a new nationalism's anti-liberal modernism cannot simply be traced to one academic. I am not claiming that. The sources of neoconservative prominence are not found in this one thinker but more in the way currents of American romanticism and contractual liberalism interact. Not all self-identified neoconservatives agree with Strauss. Moreover, Strauss is a complex philosophical mind, and his ideas can even be read as critical of some of the messianic complexes of the neoconservative leaders in the U.S. today. Nevertheless, certain key features of Strauss's political thought have been taken up by those in important positions of power in the U.S., and noting those features helps us identify the problematic features at work in today's anti-liberal modernism. Let me discuss briefly three problematic features by referring to some of Strauss's writings, citing more contemporary Straussian writers,[39] and noting some of the policies of the neoconservatives who explicitly express Straussian positions.

AVERSION TO MODERN LIBERAL DEMOCRACY

Strauss's aversion to modern liberal democracy is far more sophisticated than that of those books against liberals, featured regularly on conservative cable news channels, especially on the most popular Fox channel, where pundits like Ann Coulter rail against the "latté-slurping liberals" of the East coast. The neocons' embrace today of Strauss's critique of liberalism gains added strength, however, from the anti-liberal, conservative diatribes of pop-culture news.

Matters are also complex because Strauss can himself at times embrace something called "liberalism." In fact, he refers to his own "rational liberalism"[40] and also stresses the importance of "liberal education" in a democratic society.[41] Strauss distinguishes his liberalism, however, from that of the modern liberal democratic traditions of John Locke and John Stuart Mill, among others. Especially as this modern tradition influenced the liberalism in the founding of the U.S. government, he sees liberalism as a weak and vulnerable thing. According to Straussians, it needs "friendly criticism . . . to give it a backbone." Strauss sought to take the modern liberal tradition back to ancient political philosophy to find this backbone, to save modern liberalism from the mere "mass democracy" it is prone to become. This would be "democracy as originally meant."[42]

What is democracy as originally meant? Here emerges the troubling emphasis. For Strauss and Straussians, the purpose of democracy is not to "pander" to the masses, but to enable leadership by virtuous elites, since "democracy was meant to be an aristocracy that has broadened into a universal aristocracy."[43] The modern liberal democratic traditions of Locke, Mill, and, later, Rawls tend to be dismissed as vulnerably drifting to a low form of government in which true liberal and magnanimous figures, a gifted elite, are kept from assuming their proper role in governance.

It is a Straussian presumption, stated sometimes more baldly than at others, that the masses need an elite for effective governance. This Straussian tendency accounts for political scientist Shadia Drury's claim that, in spite of Strauss's own talk of liberalism, the effect of his notion of liberalism is really to "divest America of her liberalism." In other words, as she also writes, Strauss tends to "drive a wedge between liberalism and democracy."[44] The Straussian-informed embrace of a governing elite and suspicion of "mass democracy" easily reinforce the nondemocratic tendencies of the neocons today. Pursuing American Greatness by military might, especially from unipolarist convictions that set aside the voices of other democratic nations, is consistent with a leadership that counts on its own natural virtues and feels emboldened to act upon them without pursuing the messier processes of democratic checking and balancing.

This anti-liberal aversion may not lead to major problems in a complex national polity if it is only manifest in a few individuals. But when such individuals have built themselves into a leading academic movement of the times, have spread out through influential think tanks, and have secured appointments across several presidential administrations—as the neoconservatives and their supporters have—then the anti-liberal posture of a few individuals can become a concentrated, anti-liberal ethos of a privileged group with power. Moreover, when this ethos is also successful in garnering the support of large corporate donors, as we see today, then public life is exposed to new dangers of creating an aristocracy that is also a plutocracy, rule by the wealthy.

Straussian academic figures and others influenced by them have been at work in high offices of government throughout the last several administrations. We may note just a few of these figures:

Paul Wolfowitz (Reagan's ambassador to Indonesia, Bush Jr.'s Deputy Secretary of Defense, and now president of the World Bank), Abram Shulsky (Director of Rumsfeld and Wolfowitz's Office of Special Plans in the Defense Department), Carnes Lord (served on the National Security Council in the Reagan administration), Gary L. McDowell (advisor to Reagan's Attorney General, Edwin Meese III), Gary Schmitt (head of Reagan's National Advisory Board of Foreign Intelligence, now executive director of the Project for a New American Century [PNAC]), William Bennett (Reagan's Secretary of Education, then drug czar and author writing about values), William Kristol (Vice President Dan Quayle's Chief of Staff, now chairman of the PNAC (and editor of *The Weekly Standard*).[45] Included also are individuals throughout the powerful American Enterprise Institute, from which the Bush administration has taken many of its key leaders and from whose very auditorium Bush has announced major foreign policy moves.[46] Many who signed the 2000 document of the PNAC, *Rebuilding America's Defenses,* as well as most of the forty-one signers of a 1998 letter urging Clinton to remove Saddam Hussein from power, are Strauss-influenced neoconservatives.

With this extensive positioning of Straussian figures, there is good reason to be cautious. The Straussian aversion to liberalism and accompanying worries about "mass democracy" create not a representative elite that is often found in healthy democracies, but more a governing elite that views itself and its actions as being above the masses, and usually also above the laws of its country. Just one striking example of this is evident in the tendency of President Bush and his advisors to suspend or reinterpret international law to allow for "aggressive counter-resistance techniques" of interrogation, which amount to torture. Over 1,200 pages of official memos about interrogation and torture—as propounded by officials of the Bush regime during and after the Afghanistan and Iraq campaigns—show that "these policy makers do not like our system of justice, with its checks and balances, and rights and limits, that they have been sworn to uphold."[47]

EMBRACING DECEPTION BY GOVERNING ELITES

Critics of Strauss have highlighted his rationalization of lying and deception as necessary exercises by the virtuous elite who lead "democracy as originally meant." Drury's claim that Strauss "makes a virtue of lying and dissembling" is at the heart of her book's argument that "the pernicious influence of Leo Strauss has its source in the *kind* of elite he cultivates—an elite that is not fit for power because it is neither wise nor good."[48]

It is difficult for Drury and other critics to find outright claims in Strauss's writings where he states forthrightly that elites must lie, manipulate, or deceive.[49] It is hard, in other words, to find a statement in Strauss that quite matches Drury's summary of his position: "The philosopher-prophet [Strauss's preferred type of virtuous leader] must live a divided and duplicitous life, a life filled with deception, duplicity and subterfuge."[50]

For Straussians, though, the necessity of the virtuous elite to lie and manipulate truths must not be said openly. It is one of those truths largely fit mainly for the truly discerning. This is consistent with what scholars of Strauss call the nature of "the Straussian text." For Strauss, the best texts, the most rigorously philosophical and astute ones, are, as one former Strauss student explains, those that proffer a basic meaning that can be put out there for ordinary, average readers (an exoteric meaning), and another meaning distilled and harbored by the discerning elite (an esoteric meaning).[51] Hence, Straussians often discuss the importance of "esotericism" in reading Strauss and interpreting him. It is one of the traits that has led some to accuse Strauss and his followers of forming a quasi-religious "cult."[52] Strauss gives some momentum to the accusation by his likening of virtuous politicians' exercise of "social responsibilities" to Kabbalistic interpretation.[53] This tendency is problematic because it can easily proffer philosophical justification for a leadership elite that withholds information or filters truths for presentation to the citizenry. If this does not give outright license to lying, it certainly spreads fertile soil for the seeds of government misconduct and misrepresentation to flourish.

The rationalization and implementation of deception among policy makers can be seen at work if we refer to two key neo-con planners in the Bush regime, especially as they comported themselves in the lead-up to the U.S. assault on Iraq in March 2003. First, consider Abram Shulsky, a Strauss-influenced figure at the Department of Defense. In June 2003, as Director of the Office of Special Plans (OSP) in the U.S. Department of Defense, Shulsky was questioned by congressional reviewers about how he had put together intelligence for the case for the war on Iraq. He had come under public critique when Seymour Hersh, in the *New Yorker* magazine, analyzed Shulsky's job and described his re-examination of intelligence data from the CIA as being done "under a microscope to reveal what the intelligence community can't see." Defense Secretary Rumsfeld, Deputy Defense Secretary Wolfowitz, and Shulsky's immediate supervisor, William Luti, all believed it to be true that Saddam Hussein had weapons of mass destruction (WMDs) even though CIA information did not clearly confirm it.[54] In fact, in October 2002, CIA analysts registered doubts about the threats that the Bush regime saw in Hussein's Iraq.[55] Shulsky's job at Special Plans was to correct for the CIA's perceived failure to marshal evidence of WMDs in Iraq and of Iraq's alleged links to al-Qaeda.

If Shulsky's assignment sounds rather Straussian (allegedly massaging intelligence evidence until it met policy preferences), it should not come as a surprise because Shulsky has, himself, professed his admiration for Strauss. In addition to Deputy Secretary of Defense Paul Wolfowitz, Shulsky was a student of Strauss at the University of Chicago. Shulsky is also a co-author with Gary Schmitt of a laudatory 1999 essay on Strauss, which argues that frequently, and often by necessity, deception is "the norm in political life."[56] Moreover, Gary Schmitt was the executive director of the PNAC, which produced the 2000 document *Rebuilding America's Defenses*, arguing for the importance of U.S. forces and bases in Iraq regardless of who held power, and "even should Saddam pass from the scene."[57] Shulsky was also one of the discussants responsible for generating the PNAC document. He and his colleagues in the OSP—who "referred to themselves self-mockingly as 'the Cabal'"[58]—had long been on record advocating for regime change in Iraq, and invading the country for U.S. geopolitical interests. Their subsequent activity to remake the intelligence reports into a form that would serve a policy agenda that was never set before the American people constitutes a classic case of Straussian political elitism.

The second example we will examine of Straussian deception at work in the neocon-dominated Bush regime is Undersecretary of Defense Paul Wolfowitz, who created the Office of Special Plans that Shulsky headed. Wolfowitz's own comments show a political leader's outright embrace of deception, especially regarding administration reports about WMDs in Hussein's Iraq. Neocons' *stated* reasons for policies mattered so little that they could easily be changed if necessary. Soon after the March 2003 invasion of Iraq, Wolfowitz downplayed in May of the same year Bush's original argument about WMDs in Iraq as the reason for war, and revealed a much more convoluted alchemy of truth-telling about the extent of any threatening WMDs in Iraq prior to the U.S. assault on the Iraqi regime and civilians.[59] Still later in May 2003, he developed his point further in a radio interview. When asked then about the major reason for the preemptive assault on Iraq, as opposed to an attack on North Korea, Wolfowitz replied that the U.S. lacked the kind of economic leverage with Iraq that it can use with North Korea. North Korea could be leveraged economically, without invasion. Iraq could not be so leveraged, because its extensive oil holdings gave it more economic independence. "Look, the primary difference—to put it a little too simply—between North Korea and Iraq is that we had virtually no economic options with Iraq because the country floats on a sea of oil."[60]

Of course, if you were among those who suggested before the invasion of Iraq that the preemptive strike against Iraq was, at least in part, about the U.S. ability to have economic and political leverage through its control of oil, you were usually silenced or shunted aside as some extremist. There are, of course, simplistic ways of making the link between U.S. military campaigns and oil interests, but government and media analysts brooked almost no serious analysis of the important oil dimension. Wolfowitz's state-ment shows that the need to control oil availability and produc-tion (not just to gain oil) was a factor in the calculus, something the Bush regime never placed before the public as it did its hype about WMDs. The hyped reasons for invading Iraq could then be set aside as a fiction that had outlived its usefulness. That approach to policy justification in the public media is a clear compromise with, if not outright manifestation of, the Straussian persuasion that elites need to stand ready to deceive.

AFFIRMATION OF AGGRESSIVE NATIONALISM

Being the complex figure he is, one could actually draw from Leo Strauss a critique of the unipolar and aggressive nationalism exhib-ited among today's neoconservative policy formulators. Writ-ing in *Le Monde,* Alain Frachon and Daniel Vernet point out that Strauss would not share "the Messianic-tainted optimism that the neoconservatives bring freedom to the world."[61] Strauss did tend to teach, however, that because of the intrinsically aggressive character of human nature, citizens in a mass democracy need and benefit from powerful nationalistic sensibilities. Nationalism that often heats up aggression, as we have seen, is actually pro-pounded by Strauss as a way to focus, limit, and direct human aggression. Masses need to have their sense of citizenship culti-vated as a happiness with *their* city, with *their* nation.[62] Rulers best cultivate this nationalist sense of belonging by emphasizing citi-zens' unity with one another against external threats. The born ruler will, in fact, exacerbate this sense of threat, the tendency toward enmity between states, and thus "must have strong war-like functions."[63]

Defenders of Strauss might point out that he emphasized that the ideal wise man pursues "a transpolitical justice, the justice which is irreconcilable with hurting anyone." But such a wise man, according to Strauss, is usually not a ruler. In fact, advises Strauss, it is best that wise men *not* rule. It is "the unwise" who should rule, though "under law."[64] In other words, Strauss leaves little room between the necessary rule by the unwise and the impossible transpolitical utopia of rule by the wise. This leaves his readers with a world of politics where rulers rule through aggressive, war-like functions that set nation against nation.

It is not surprising, then, that the contemporary U.S. neoconservatives who cite Strauss often rationalize an aggressive nationalism and idealize the links between war and what they believe to be an effective foreign policy. Irving Kristol, the godfather of neoconservatism, recently thanked Leo Strauss, along with Donald Kagan (the co-chair with Gary Schmitt of the *Rebuilding America's Defenses* document), for instilling in the U.S. nation-state a set of patriotic attitudes. After stressing that patriotism is a natural, healthy, and "powerful American sentiment," especially in the present situation of U.S. imperial responsibility, Kristol calls American "statesmen" to their primary role, that is, "to distinguish friends from enemies." This enables the current United States, he says, to pursue its "ideological" identity, a benign one, of course: "to defend, if possible a democratic nation under attack from nondemocratic forces, external or internal" (he mentions here the need to defend France, Britain, and Israel).[65]

Six years ago, Drury summarized well what is dangerous about this aggressive nationalism in the neoconservative dream:

> Kristol's nationalism not only encourages a belligerent foreign policy, it assumes that American values are the only true values. This highly presumptuous attitude ignores the plurality of human groups and civilizations. It rejects plurality as a slippery slope to relativism and nihilism. . . . Kristol's nationalism not only invites an aggressive foreign policy, it also destabilizes domestic politics by depicting it in terms of the distinction between friend and foe—the enemies of the nation and the friends of Sleeping Beauty. This dualistic mentality has the effect of turning the political contest for power into an all out war. . . . When political opponents are demonized, simple ambition is reinforced and politicians are tempted to overstep the bounds of law. When domestic politics is turned into a contest between the forces of good and the forces of evil, when political opponents are regarded as the enemies of civilization, the results are dishonest political tactics, corruption, and conflict.[66]

In sum, a contractual liberalism that strikes an alliance with American romanticism, as it increasingly has in the post-9/11 moment, becomes still more problematic, with its transformation into anti-liberal modernism. The largest, most powerful governing apparatus of modernity is now being shaped and guided by those who have managed, through anti-liberal movements in the academy and society, to separate liberalism out from the modern systems with which liberalism has long been associated. Again, that liberalism, conjoined with forms of Western modernity, was always highly problematic, resulting continually in the constraints of *contractual* liberalism. Severe and ruthless as this liberalism could be (especially for indigenous peoples, for those caught up in centuries of slavery, and for those ground under by relentless forces of colonialism and neocolonialism), repressed peoples could sometimes make use of the liberal ethos to open up modernity, transforming it in some liberating ways. The emergence and growth of the U.S. Republic, its Constitution and Bill of Rights, its "creed," together with civic nationalism and the extension of voting rights to African Americans and women, are all cases of struggling peoples using liberal society's announced commitments to mitigate some of modernity's worst faults.

With liberalism split off from modernism, especially in the Bush regime of the early-twenty-first-century United States, modernity's worst can show itself again, and this already is evident in the way currents in the post-9/11 USA have created a unipolar world affected by U.S. hegemony and a state of perpetual war (the "war on terror").

If we wanted a historical analogy for understanding our times, one offered by Michael Lind's analysis of the Bush regime may be especially helpful. Drawing on the work of sociologist and economist Thorstein Veblen, Lind likens the present nationalist moment to the Wilhelmine period before the first World War, when Germany's powerful industrial state and the extraordinary governing apparatus it featured came under the control of "a reactionary, aristocratic caste" known as the "Prussian Junkers," who controlled German governance in the late nineteenth and early twentieth centuries.[67] Lind, who is from Texas, traces the power of the Bush regime to the political history of landed, aristocratic groups in the U.S. South in *Made in Texas*. Even though past federal government programs (the New Deal, for example) rebuilt much of the Old South, those from Southern oligarchic caste cultures now wield their oligarchic power over the vast, modern technological apparatus of the nation. Lind writes, "the new technologies created by Silicon Valley and other modes of high-tech capitalism in the United States are being put to imperial uses by a military-political elite of rich Southerners and their allies who think of world politics in premodern terms of foreign resource extraction (the hoped-for American conquest of Middle Eastern oil fields) or the exploitation of politically powerless foreign labor (the sweatshop approach to globalization and immigration)."[68]

Lind's most powerful insight is that, like the situation of the Prussian Junker elite in Germany, the U.S. industrial-technological state is in the hands of anti-liberal oligarchic powers. I suspect he may overplay the Southernness of the U.S. elite; after all, the South's political power, especially vis-à-vis issues of slavery and racism, was often tolerated and perpetuated by Northern elites and workers. Today's anti-liberal elite is best traced to the currents of American romanticism and contractual liberalism as they have newly come alive from the 9/11 moment and combined in especially threatening ways.

Nevertheless, Lind's historical analogy is suggestive, if not exact. It helps us focus on the anti-liberal modernism posed by Bush and his supporters in a period when religious and secular revolutionary American romanticisms are uniting with contractual liberalism. "It remains to be seen whether the Southern militarists of the Republican party, by reckless strategy of imperial over-extension, will accidentally destroy the American empire they are trying to create and suffer the unlamented fate of the British imperial office corps, the Prussian Junkers, and the Japanese samurai."[69]

How the fate of U.S. hegemony is played out historically may depend on working out another specter—not American romanticism in its religious and secular forms, nor contractual liberalism, but prophetic spirit, a specter to counter the specters of empire.

5

THE SPECTER OF PROPHETIC SPIRIT

Don't the necessary weapons reside precisely within the
creative and prophetic power of the multitude?

—MICHAEL HARDT AND ANTONIO NEGRI, *EMPIRE*

The specters of U.S. empire in the forms of American
romanticism and contractual liberalism may bedevil its republic,
the diverse global humanity, and our ecological biosphere. Yet
another specter will require a reckoning. It is the specter of prophetic spirit, with its unique capacities, through peoples' movements and everyday practices, to engage, counter, and redirect
the forces of American romanticism and contractual liberalism.

In this chapter, we will need to ask two important questions: (1) What way of being is consonant with prophetic spirit?
and (2) What are the means by which prophetic spirit's way of
being relates to American romanticism and contractual liberalism? Understanding that relation will mean showing how prophetic spirit resists and reframes both the belonging being that
is distorted by American romanticism and the expectant being
that is distorted in contractual liberalism. Prophetic spirit's major
contribution to public life after 9/11 consists in its reworking of
belonging being and expectant being.

Prophetic spirit counters and reworks the being of the other
two specters of empire by the strength emanating from its own
way of being. Our first task, then, is to understand prophetic spirit's way of being.

PROPHETIC SPIRIT AS
BROADENING AND DEEPENING BEING

In its simplest form, being "prophetic," as noted by Cornel West, one of our era's most profound prophetic voices, is marked by "human deeds of justice and kindness that attend to the unjust sources of human hurt and misery." Prophetic being's utterances have as their "especial aim . . . to shatter deliberate ignorance and willful blindness to the suffering of others and to expose the clever forms of evasion and escape we devise in order to hide and conceal injustice." West portrays the "goal" of prophetic work as being "to stir up in us the courage to care and empower us to change our lives and our historical circumstances."[1]

West's words are judicious and eloquent formulations of prophetic function in confronting injustice, exposing evil, challenging indifference, shattering ignorance and evasion, and so on. Many people, especially those from the great prophetic religions, will recognize West's phrasing as eloquent restatements of the power and value of the prophetic.

Here, I am pushing further this notion of the prophetic and asking a key question: From what way of being do all this critical work and speech derive? I propose that prophetic spirit is birthed from and sustained by what I will call "broadening and deepening being." This is a slightly more abstract kind of discourse, but it is helpful for identifying how the prophetic function lives not only in religious traditions but also as a publicly available social practice. Prophetic spirit is a way of being that is always at work broadening and deepening the horizons of our lives and, in the process, giving rise to ever new awareness of breadth and depth in our understandings of being.

As my choice of metaphors reveals, prophetic spirit, thus understood, integrates a largely spatial, multidimensional vision into its observation and analysis of history. As we shall see, this "spatial" mode attends to the places and social spaces in which historical agents and processes take place. By contrast, the belonging being of romanticism and the expectant being of contractual liberalism tend to lead with discourses more shaped by a temporal consciousness running along an axis from past to present. Along that axis, belonging being tends, in the language of Paul Tillich, to be oriented to "the whence," the "from where" of life and being. It is backward-leaning, we might say, and thus belonging being tends to spawn romanticisms. Whether they are conservative or revolutionary, religious or secular in nature, they revere origins. Along the temporal axis, there develops also an expectant being as orientation to "the whither," the "where to" of life and being. Here, breaks from tradition are made; critical rationality and desires for new freedom seek to evolve from older traditions of thought and practice, or at least claim to do so.[2] Romanticism and contractual liberalism, belonging being and expectant being, are primarily ways of being shaped by temporality. Western theories of being, ontologies, have usually privileged the rhetorics of temporal consciousness, whether forged by religious minds that see life played out from divine creation to divine future consummation, or by more secular minds touting progress or, more pessimistically, musing on human being-toward-death.

Prophetic spirit's broadening and deepening being is not without a temporal awareness of the whence and whither of humanity and creation. Indeed, prophetic spirit's own expectation of a future epoch when justice will flourish, as in Judaism, Christianity, and Islam, has often helped spur movements that broke free from "the old" so as to move temporally toward the new. Tillich argued precisely this in *The Socialist Decision*.[3]

Nevertheless, prophetic spirit's consciousness is more shaped by spatial discourses than it is by temporal ones, or, better, it analyzes human movement through time by looking through lenses that broaden and deepen our views of temporal life. The broadening and deepening being of prophetic spirit takes in the temporal axis by which romanticism and liberalism orient themselves, but then clothes that axis in considerations of greater complexity. In this way, broadening and deepening being creates prophetic spirit's unique view of history, discerning spatial dimensions (broader realms, deeper levels, encompassing wholes) within historical life. Let us trace more specifically how this broadening and deepening yields the distinctive concerns of prophetic spirit.

BREADTH

As to breadth, prophetic spirit sees history as markedly social. History's forward-moving character is, to be sure, not denied. Prophetic spirit, though, stresses that history's moving forward happens not just by means of some posited historical impetus or force of progress but by various kinds of dynamic interplay between social groups (conflict and antagonism as well as cooperation and coordination). Prophetic spirit scans, for example, the manifold of social group dynamics, discerning and seeing history as a broad field where some groups with minorities hold power and occupy centers while others are consigned, as in so many concentric circles, to outlying spheres, each more peripheral to the center than the last. Peripheral groups, such as dependent colonies, find it necessary to circulate around the powerful centers like London, for example, in the British Empire. Prophetic spirit cultivates breadth through a vision that discerns centers and peripheries. Neither center nor radical periphery is static; they may often be in flux, with members in each exchanging positions. Moreover, prophetic spirit, as it develops ever more complex analyses, moves beyond simplistic dichotomies of center versus periphery, exploring the many different ways in which those at the periphery and those with the power of the center interact in multiple ways, often in close proximity to one another. Nevertheless, these more complex analyses often depend on the meaningfulness of the distinction. It is intrinsic to the broad concern of prophetic spirit to be attuned both to the ways of power at the center and, especially, to suffering under exploitative power among the most peripheral, marginalized groups.

Often it is the marginalized ones at the edges who most frequently generate this prophetic breadth of vision. About African American women, for example, bell hooks writes: "Living as we did—on the edge—we developed a particular way of seeing reality. We looked both from the outside in and from the inside out. We focused our attention on the center as well as on the margin. We understood both. This mode of seeing reminded us of the existence of a whole universe, a main body made up of both margin and center."[4] To use this kind of social lens on historical formations is to cultivate the broadening vision at work in prophetic spirit's way of being.

DEPTH

Prophetic spirit also has another analytic, one that focuses on the depth dimension of historical life. By this I mean that prophetic spirit discerns that our temporal existence is textured also by different levels of life, according to which there are different strata of power and empowerment. Prophetic spirit thus is acutely aware of how humans form hierarchies differentiating the high and the low, the social spaces lying above and below one another. History's move forward, then, is viewed by prophetic spirit as achieved by various groups' exercise of domination, repression, or oppression "over" others, and of others' resistance to them. The very narrating of history, and the writing of history books, is often itself the work of those "on top" who win history's power struggles, and who then tell it to flatter themselves or to rationalize their governing agendas. Prophetic spirit's vision and discernment are marked by sensitivity to hierarchy. It sees not only the upper echelons (upper classes, the overclass) but also, especially, those at the lower rungs of hierarchy (lower classes, the underclass). It focuses on the "underside of history," to recall Dietrich Bonhoeffer's well-known phrase. Its concerns are with the underclass—low-income groups, the lower class, the oppressed, the repressed, the dominated. Each of these terms may be given distinctive meanings by the analysts of prophetic spirit, but all are variations on prophetic spirit's attentiveness to levels of hierarchical structure.

As an example of prophetic spirit's way of viewing with a deepening visionary power, note military historian Chalmers Johnson's description of a U.S. Navy aircraft carrier. He could have told the story of U.S. empire and recent naval campaigns by plotting the temporal occurrence of battles and geopolitical events in the epochal unfolding of naval history. But instead he pauses to offer this description of life aboard the USS Kitty Hawk:

Boarding [the ship] is like entering a time warp back to the former Deep South. In the bowels of the carrier, where the crews
are cooped up for six months at a time, manual workers sleep
dozens to a room. Most are Black or Puerto Rican, paid $7,000
to $10,000 a year to work in the broiling temperatures of the
kitchens and engine rooms. As you move up the eleven segregated levels towards the pilot's quarters beneath the deck, the
living quarters become larger, the air cooler, and the skin tones
lighter. Officers exist in almost total ignorance of the teeming
world beneath them, passing around second-hand tales of mur-
ders, gang fights, and drug abuse. Visitors are banned from ven-
turing down to the lowest decks, which swelter next to the vast
nuclear-powered engines. . . . Access to the flight deck, which
buzzes with F-14 and F-18 aircraft taking part in exercises, is
banned for all except the flight crew.[5]

Here amid a military historian's work is prophetic spirit's vision,
a deepening consciousness of history's events surfacing the pain of
those, quite literally, on the underside of history.

At its best, the visions and analyses of prophetic spirit draw
from both the metaphors of breadth (the social structuring created by exclusion) and those of depth (hierarchical structures created by structures of gender, class, race, or other domination) in
order to describe and explain the lives and livelihoods of those
who are dominated and excluded. Suffering has been a hallmark
of the contexts of the dominated and excluded, and it is from
these contexts that prophetic spirit's vision has often been forged,
for reasons that are clear from bell hooks's comments above. By
contrast, as numerous studies have shown, those at the centers or
pinnacles of systems usually do not need to attend to the peripheries and—even when they do, out of a need to control them
or to maintain dominance over them, or, sometimes to assist in
their "development"—peripheral or subjugated groups are rarely
accorded the status of fully human historical agents. Suffering
people on the margins are not really seen by those at centers and
pinnacles of power. It is the socially excluded and hierarchically
dominated ones who have seen, from their vantage points of suffering, the more spatial texturing of historical being and its dif-
ferential levels of power.[6] From that seeing, prophetic spirit is

born and sustained. Others might seek an "authentic solidarity" with the socially dominated and excluded,[7] but prophetic spirit's root and power emanates from movements among those who see it most clearly because they suffer it most intensely.

Prophetic spirit's mode of being, then, is primarily a spatial one dwelling in the tensions arising from hierarchical domination and social exclusion, especially mindful of those that Hebrew, Christian, and Muslim prophetic voices deemed "the poor, the orphaned, the widow, and the needy."[8] This group of paramount concern to prophetic spirit may also be deemed the "proletariat," provided that notion is freed from the somewhat limited reference it had in the work of Karl Marx and especially among later Marxists who used it mainly to refer to a predominantly male, industrial working-class group. That is a constraint on the notion of the proletariat that is particularly egregious, given the term's roots as referring to those "reserved only to beget children," thus reflecting "the devalorization of women's labor of reproduction."[9] As many thinkers have stressed, the term "proletariat" needs to be expanded not only to include devalued reproductive labor and the work of poor women (often not even counted in standard measures of national income, economic growth, and productivity[10]), but also to take in the whole "class" of humanity that so often remains anonymous and nameless—traditionally proletarian and lumpen proletarian, landless and expropriated, the multitude of diverse poor, those criminalized for being poor, terrorized and subject to coercion, female and male of all ages.[11]

PROPHETIC SPIRIT AFTER 9/11

What form might prophetic spirit's way of being take, given the 9/11 moment? What might be the effect of broadening and deepening being in the land of the USA, after the historic and mythic repercussions of 9/11 have rippled through the personal, social, political, and economic lives of U.S. residents?

It is in the wake of 9/11 that prophetic spirit's way of being can make a significant contribution, orienting public life and values in new ways. Prophetic spirit's practice, while shaped by a continual vision of the breadth and depth of history, is always a potential specter—a haunting of the present order of things, birthing transformation from the lives of those abandoned by centers of power, pushed to the margins, and ground down and held down by higher powers.

After 9/11, plates in the U.S. social terrain have been forced to shift, and the accompanying repercussions of this shifting might bring forth prophetic spirit as an even greater spectral force. Prophetic spirit does have a foreboding and ominous character, but instead of threatening U.S. public life with more specters of empire (as American romanticism and contractual liberalism long have done and do today) prophetic spirit is a threat to those imperial constructs themselves, engaging them and transforming them. In so doing, prophetic spirit's foreboding, its threat, is also a way to life and flourishing, toward a counterimperial vision and practice.

The two concluding chapters of this book show how prophetic spirit might break forth as a rival spectral force, one full of hope. The crisis of renewed strength and destructive power of romanticism and liberalism in the 9/11 moment can be an opportunity for prophetic spirit. In challenging and reorienting American romanticism, prophetic spirit yields what I will discuss in chapter 6 as a hope-filled specter of "revolutionary belonging" for U.S. residents. In challenging and reorienting contractual liberalism, prophetic spirit offers what I discuss in chapter 7 as a new sense of "revolutionary expectation."

The final two chapters of this book, then, fill out what it is that prophetic spirit might become in post-9/11 USA, and complete the notion of prophetic spirit described here in chapter 5. As will become clear from those important concluding chapters, my proposals for prophetic spirit after 9/11 in the United States are rooted in already existing, albeit repressed and marginalized, cultural practices. Prophetic spirit can thrive anew because it is carried today by its own kind of undying revolutionary tradition, which generates revolutionary expectation. These resources have not been absent in the post-9/11 era. Immediately after the attacks on the World Trade Center and the Pentagon, many citizens took to the streets, even in New York City neighborhoods, to raise their cries against vengeful counter-attacks by the U.S. in Afghanistan, and especially against Iraq.[12] "Not in Our Name" was a rallying cry around which many of prophetic spirit mobilized.[13] Massively organized world public opinion against the impending 2003 war on Iraq was referred to as one of the "two superpowers" along with the United States.[14] High school and college students risked suspension and criticism for being disloyal and unpatriotic in their denunciations of U.S. war-making.[15] Artists and singers have mobilized repeatedly against imperial war designs of the U.S.[16] Religious leaders, theologians, and people of faith tapped into their prophetic religious traditions to register their criticism and outrage over the imperial mélange of ever worsening U.S. practices of torture, war, and occupation.[17] All of these efforts, and more, signal and make possible the thriving of prophetic spirit's tradition of resistance, a resistance with senses of revolutionary belonging and expectation that we will explore more fully in the final two chapters. But before turning to those chapters, let us attend to the notion of "spirit" that can be seen to persist at the animating center of such movements.

THE PROPHETIC AS "SPIRIT"

In the case of spirit, freedom prevails over
determination, and the underivably new is created.[18]

—PAUL TILLICH, *SYSTEMATIC THEOLOGY*

On the basis of the foregoing explication of prophetic spirit, we are in a better position to understand why I have referred to the prophetic as "spirit" throughout this book. It should be clear that even though the roots of the term "prophetic"—along with "prophets," "prophetism," and "prophecy"—lie in religious traditions that speak of God and Spirit, I do not propose that the "spirit" of prophetic spirit means that we must necessarily proceed to a discourse on God or to notions of "divine spirit." Nor, as I assume is even more clearly the case, does prophetic spirit refer to one of many "spirits" that are believed to reside on some plane above or beyond the kinds of human practices and histories I am addressing in this book. No, as I stated in the introduction, prophetic spirit is a function that can also be alive *in* secular social criticism when it speaks to power about weaker and repressed groups of society, or serves as sentinel, discerning trends and offering warnings about the plight of the body politic. Prophetic spirit, then, is a profoundly human dimension of the cultural and historical practices constituting social life.

Yet the question persists: Why refer to the prophetic as "spirit"? Why not just discuss the prophetic as another form of cultural and historical unfolding, leaving the notion of "spirit" aside as just too misleading—because in English, unlike German, for one example, it is not readily understood as human, so it almost automatically connotes the presence of divinity, or of God.

The reason I preserve the term at all lies in the fact that it enables reflection on a particular kind of cultural-historical experience and function that warrants special attention. In this sense, this work on prophetic spirit is a plea to use the notion of "spirit" to refer to important dimensions of culture and history that are very much human, but dimensions to which little attention is usually given. The term "spirit" features etymologies that relate it to "breath"—as in *pneuma* (Greek), *spiritus* (Latin), *Geist* (German), *ruach* (Hebrew), and most Indo-Germanic languages. With this connection to breath, spirit has been seen as the power of life, the vital animating pulse of life, the dynamic that keeps life living, as it were, in a rhythm that is vital and revitalizing through the multiplicity of breaths, breathing. To recall this etymology is to revive a notion of spirit that is not opposite to matter but intrinsic to it— an animating vitality of sensuous earth, a dynamic at work in the biological, historical, cultural, and social powers of earth.[19] This spirit is a dimension of human life where the new emerges (the next breath), and in a way that maintains the continuity of a certain form of life (the breathing being). Both the new breath and the continuation of the being that breathes (a continuation made possible by the new breath) are crucial for human freedom as a kind of flourishing related to the occurrence of the new. We might say that prophetic spirit is as essential to social life as breathing is to biological life. Without prophetic spirit's broadening and deepening way of being, social life narrows, thins, shrivels, and dies.

What more can be said about this vitalizing newness that is "spirit" in the politics and culture of earth? Paul Tillich tried to become more specific by turning to the cultural creation of Shakespeare's *Hamlet* to give an example of how spirit births the new in human culture. In so doing, he reflects on how very earthy, social dynamics, which constitute spirit's creativity, seem to birth something "underivably new" in human history. "In the creation of *Hamlet* by Shakespeare the material, particular form, personal presuppositions, occasioning factors, and so on, are derivable. All these elements are effective in the artistic process which created *Hamlet*, but the result is new in the sense of *the underivable*. . . . The new is not bound to the individual substance, but it rises out of the substance and has effects on the character of the substance."[20] The new that is the hallmark of spirit emerges not on a supernatural plane above or beyond nature, culture, and history, but within a configuration of natural, cultural, and historical qualities that occasion the emergence of a creative form that has traits leading us to say, somewhat strangely, perhaps, that it is "underivable," even though derived from, emergent from within any number of other very specific conditions.

As the epigraph by Tillich for this section shows, Tillich views the emergence of "the underivable" as a flourishing of "freedom over determination," a strange prevailing of freedom that becomes hallmark of "spirit" in the human dimension of life. Other scholars have proceeded in similar fashion.

Psychologist and cultural historian Joel Kovel, for example, working independently from Tillich, also links the "spirit" to selves and groups that have a freeing experience within history. This freedom may be from the bondage of a divided self or an imprisoned self, or from forces that repress and oppress a historical group. In his tellingly titled book *History and Spirit: An Inquiry into the Philosophy of Liberation*, Kovel, a Marxist, is not writing of divine spirit, but human spirit—spirit as a complex dimension of cultural-historical existence. For him, spirit is that dynamic dimension in human creative being where one experiences emergence of the new as an event that is freeing. One is continually entering into freer space, enjoying breathing room, as it were, when one is steeped in spirit, which is creativity enhanced by emancipation. Precisely how creativity and emancipation interplay to generate hope will be discussed more in chapter 7.

The prophetic is spirit, then, not as divine Spirit or as a kind of being in some metacultural or metahistorical realm; the prophetic is spirit as a distinctive configuration of cultural and historical conditions that enable creative emergence of emancipation. Prophetic spirit, while not always focused on empires, has had a special emancipating function in resisting them if for no other reason than, as historian Norman Etherington observed, because imperialism, our struggles with it, and our theories about it "have a rare power to carry us up to the mountaintop where we seem to see meaningful patterns formed by the incessant to-ings and fro-ings of iniquitous mankind on the plain below."[21] Imperial regimes deal modes of confinement and destruction that are both comprehensive and complex in their dynamics, often compounding military and national power plays with racial, sexual, economic, and ethnocentric ones. Imperial regimes thus set a dramatic backdrop for the human spirit's need for breath, for freedom, for the new.

In previous research into the way the term "spirit" functions in cultural configurations, I argued that spirit has, in addition to its meanings of freedom and liberation, an "integrative" set of meanings.[22] It involves a kind of vision or sensibility that reaches for holistic perspective, seeking unity among disparate parts of one's being and reality, seeking and sensing unseen dimensions and possibilities. This holistic vision of spirit rarely rivals the prevalence of liberation or freedom in discourses of spirit, but it often accompanies drives for liberation.

In this book, the prophetic may pertain primarily to spirit as emancipatory—under imperial constraints—but prophetic spirit here also has this holistic orientation. Thus it concerns an emancipation not just vis-à-vis empire but also regarding other forms of injustice bound up with it. This holism is suggested by the very term I have used to characterize prophetic spirit's way of being, "broadening and deepening being." It has a multidimensional apprehension of life that is historical, looking to origins and to futures in expectation, but it attains a special complexity because it uses its broadening vision to apprehend and analyze groups marginalized from centers and its deepening vision for attending to groups subordinated at lower levels of hierarchical systems. In this breadth and depth of vision is a drive for integrative vision, a move toward more comprehensive wholes, another element of human spirit.

In the post-9/11 USA, the prophetic mode's broadening and deepening being seeks to promote types of belonging being and expectant being that are both more comprehensive and more complex than those found in American romanticism and contractual liberalism. Thus prophetic spirit, across the next two chapters, is articulated as "revolutionary belonging" and "revolutionary expectation." Prophetic spirit's revolutionary mode of belonging being explodes the American romanticists' fixation on founding fathers and founding documents and analyzes and reveres the fluctuating and pulsating worlds of everyday people—rebelling, organizing, marching, sometimes rioting, but more often taking everyday steps of resistance—who laid the revolutionary conditions for the founding fathers' partially revolutionary efforts. Similarly, prophetic spirit's revolutionary mode of expectation is more comprehensive and complex than contractual liberalism, exploding its truncated and limited discourses of liberty and equality by mobilizing leaders of marginalized and repressed groups, and their supporters, as agents who can artfully plan and vigilantly craft a truly radical liberalism.

It is in this kind of engagement of American romanticism and contractual liberalism that the prophetic is a spirit that comes as emancipatory practice. Prophetic spirit even has a "transcendent" power—not as going above or outside culture and history but as being a configuration of culture and history in and through which something new, something creatively "underivable," is looked for. The prophetic's way of being is a cultural and historical *spirit,* enabling an emancipatory transcendence of empire's romanticism and liberalism. Thus prophetic spirit becomes itself a specter to empire. We are prepared now to see how it restores a revolutionary belonging to U.S. citizens and how it nurtures a revolutionary expectation.

6

REVOLUTIONARY BELONGING

These sheep, simple as they are, cannot be pulled as
heretofore. In short, there is no ruling them; and now,
to leave the metaphor, the heads of the mobility
grow dangerous to the gentry; and how to
keep them down is the question. . . .

—"FOUNDING FATHER" GOUVERNEUR MORRIS,
ON OBSERVING CROWD PROTESTS ON THE EVE OF THE
FIRST AMERICAN REVOLUTION (C. 1774)

"These sheep" are still the strength of any government that would enable a flourishing of the peoples of the United States and of the lands and other nations living under U.S. influence. Prophetic spirit challenges American romanticism with a deeper and broader patriotism. Prophetic spirit sees into the realms behind the so-called founding fathers of the American Revolution, prior to their imposed restraints on the aspirations of diverse peoples clamoring for new freedoms. Prophetic spirit offers a new romance for today's residents of the United States of America, a romance not celebrating founding fathers, who were a gentrified class of entitled white property owners, a romance that remembers and reveres what Gouverneur Morris observed when he warned: "the heads of the mobility grow dangerous to the gentry." Morris's reference to "the mobility" may be a strange one in modern English, but it ably connotes the dynamic, insurgent, ever moving, and never static qualities that mark a group of people who, in more vernacular terms of today, are "on the move," bent on change. This mobility, as we will unfold it in this chapter, involves a diverse set of freedom movements ongoing around the rim of the Atlantic Ocean, including Caribbean, Mesoamerican, and South American groups, involving European, African, indigenous, Asian, and other peoples of many backgrounds. Prophetic spirit thus does not deny the belonging being that seeks to mythologize our origins, upon which American romanticism fixates and then distorts. Its broader and deeper envisioning, though, reorients American belonging to those peoples marginalized and put down by the currents of American romanticism, but in whom have long lived the motions and movements of revolutionary change.

Prophetic spirit's revolutionary belonging will be a strange and difficult one, even if, as I believe, it is where a tradition of renewing hope is to be found. American belonging, if it is to be revolutionary in the ways we most need in post-9/11 USA, and in a manner to rival the virulent romanticisms of our day, must take a special fluid form and so become spirited. Prophetic spirit orients human drives for belonging, not primarily to founders and structures, but to a mobility, to that "mobility that grows dangerous to gentry." By my use of "gentry," I mean not just an upper class marked by family dynasty, wealth, and power, but all groups that display not only class, but also race, gender, nationality, or other categories as markers of entitlement to claim a high status that is detrimental to others' freedoms. Prophetic spirit's way of being forges American belonging anew, as a belonging to the fluctuating, freedom-seeking, everyday people who must take on those among the "gentry" who would deprive the many of their freedoms.

Can a nation's people belong to such a fluid "mobility"? I grant it is difficult to imagine; perhaps it is even harder to practice. U.S. citizens are usually accustomed to revere a revolutionary heritage beginning with founding fathers. Especially the romanticizing strict constructionists among us also cultivate their revolutionary heritage by making a near fetish of the Declaration of Independence or of the U.S. Constitution, both interpreted, so it is advised, "as the founding fathers intended." Romanticist fixation on the father figures and on their written documents, however, overlooks the fact that both founders and founding documents drew their power not from themselves but from a revolutionary mobility among the populace. Moreover, as Morris's statement shows, these founders feared, sought to limit, and often betrayed that originating, revolutionary mobility. Morris was one of the founders who opposed the U.S. Constitution's early protection of slavery but more numerous others among the founding gentry won out.[1] In this sense, American founders betrayed the abolitionist winds that blew in the revolutionary storm that birthed the Constitution. But who makes up the mobility to which democratic peoples belong? Whether we can imagine or practice a belonging to a revolutionary mobility may depend on having a clearer grasp of it.

The mobility that is at the heart of prophetic spirit's revolutionary belonging in America can be brought into clearer focus by viewing it in three ways: (1) as a new revolutionary acting subject in history, (2) as a distinctive revolutionary tradition, and (3) as a revolutionary mythic language. Further, how this revolutionary sense of belonging gets practiced will require our move into the final chapter on revolutionary expectation. Here, though, we begin with prophetic spirit's way of belonging.

REVOLUTIONARY SUBJECT

The revolutionary mobility that prophetic spirit highlights is marked first by a different revolutionary subject: the active historical force, the primary agent of change that gives birth to revolutionary being. A first clue as to who or what this subject is comes from the very nature of prophetic spirit as we have already discussed it. As being that is broadening and deepening, with an analytic vision that runs wide to the margin and cuts deep to expose hierarchies and inequalities, prophetic spirit yields a correspondingly distinctive kind of revolutionary subject.

Not surprisingly, this active subject is difficult to bring into focus. Not only is it generally a nonelite group (though often elites can also work in support of the revolutionary subject), it is also diverse, drawing from a range as multiple and varied as the masses left marginalized and oppressed by history's ruling groups.

In U.S. history, about whom are we speaking? Again, the revolutionary subject is not made up only, or even primarily, of the Jeffersons, Adams, Washingtons, and Franklins. These figures were more observers of the powerful motivating forces in their times than the key revolutionary subjects themselves. U.S. historians Peter Linebaugh and Marcus Rediker have referred to the revolutionary subject as a "motley crew." This phrase was used often in the period of the American Revolution, but Linebaugh and Rediker formalize it and propose that the motley crew (or, better, motley crews) was the real revolutionary subject, the engine of revolutionary transformation, or "an actual coordination"[2] of resistance activities that gave rise to revolutionary change. It was this work of the motley crew that Samuel Adams not only observed but also transformed into political theories that eventually would be used to justify rebellion against the British crown.

In Adams's time, sailors resisted by rioting and fleeing the efforts of ship captains to impress them into service. Adams observed slave uprisings in the South and Caribbean and wrote for over two years about them in his weekly publication, *The Independent Advertiser*. He saw men and women, boys and girls, ruffians, and a few abolitionist preachers stirring a revolutionary cauldron. As a well-educated descendent of white settlers, Adams, like Morris, trembled when watching these unruly masses boil to the surface in the colonies of the late eighteenth century. He, too, saw them as "sheep" but knew there would be no controlling them, so he gave voice to their turbulent uprisings. As Linebaugh and Rediker tell it, as a young propagandist for rebellion against England, Adams could not simply watch a motley crew of "Africans, Scotsmen, Dutchmen, Irishmen and Englishmen battle the press-gang and then describe them as being engaged simply in the struggle for the rights of Englishmen."[3] No, he was forced by observing the diversity of the many rebels to write about the rights of "the people"— this latter term being the one employed by the many ship crews to refer to themselves as the group forced into a common labor aboard the empire's ships. The discourse of a revolutionary people claiming rights by a common humanity has its roots in the motley crew's rising together for redress of diverse grievances (against forced impressment, slavery, tyranny, and other abuses).

Revolutionary belonging in America means counting our-selves among this motley crew. "Motley crew" does not mean a randomly selected, spontaneous hodgepodge of individuals. To be sure, the diversity in the motley crew at work on America's eastern seaboard was striking, even stirring, with its members drawn from cultural worlds all around the Atlantic rim: runaway slaves from Africa, the Caribbean, and the American South; women and men from the lower classes of Naples, London, Paris, Charlestown, and New York; Native Americans having diverse bonds of kin or common interest with all the above, as well as suffering their dramatic loss of lands and peoples.[4] Asians, too, found their way into the motley crew, especially as they were funneled early into the Americas' Atlantic system through labor systems of the Caribbean.[5]

But for all this diversity, the motley crew had a definitive shape that was born of those times. It was a collective produced by long-existing, routine practices of forced labor—on the plantations and in the maritime ships, both of which serviced emergent European "modernity" or "the modern colonial world system," as Walter Mignolo rightly insists we call it.[6] The labor demands on planta-tions and ships were the forces that both powered the empires of the day and created the groups that resisted those empires.

The motley crew, then, was a collected labor force that, under the pains of imperial subjugation, forged a collective life of resis-tance. These were largely sailors and soldiers, but they also included various commoners—men and women forced off of lands expropriated by powerful new classes around the rim of the Atlantic. Native Americans and other indigenous peoples entered the mix, as did many pirates who, in spite of history's caricature of them as only lawless barbarians against civilization, actually displayed creative collective genius that sought to defy the com-mercial elite and their colonial dreams.[7]

So the motley crew was the revolutionary subject of the Amer-ican Revolution, the dynamic group of actors who made it possible. Linebaugh and Rediker summarize the mobility about which Morris warned: "At the peak of revolutionary possibility, the motley crew appeared as a synchronicity or an actual coordination among the 'risings of the people' of the port cities, the resistance of African American slaves, and Indian struggles on the frontier."[8]

Such a motley crew was at work in the formative events so often recounted in U.S. history textbooks. Participants in the Boston Tea Party included indentured servants active all around the Atlantic rim, often between London and Boston. The crowds who suffered the British soldiers' gunfire at the Boston Massacre of 1770 included boys and ruffians, servants and slaves.

But the erasure of this revolutionary motley crew began early: when craftsman Paul Revere rendered the massacre as an engraving, he "tried to render the 'motley rabble' respectable by leaving black faces out of the crowd and putting in entirely too many gentlemen."[9] Prophetic spirit's romance with America's revolutionary origins does not tolerate that erasure; it celebrates that revolutionary crowd's full, diverse humanity. The belonging being of this revolutionary subject does not romance soil, nation, or polity but celebrates the mobility and movement of diverse peoples struggling to orient soil, nation, and polity toward full and just inclusion in a common life.

REVOLUTIONARY TRADITION

Such a revolutionary subject, which birthed the founding of the U.S., had a history. The motley crew has a tradition. It stretches back to at least 1640, when, during the English Revolution, prophets, preachers, and visionary resisters of many stripes organized themselves and their comrades in protest and resistance to the emergence of modern colonial capitalism. This revolutionary tradition also stretches forward into our time. Identifying today's bearers of revolutionary tradition is a task postponed until the final chapter of this book. Here, in order to focus prophetic spirit's transformation of American romanticist belonging into a revolutionary belonging in America, I limit myself to discussion of the times antedating and preparing the way for the revolution that emancipated the colonies from Britain.

We have already noted how the founding fathers' prominence in the 1770s and 1780s was dependent upon a revolutionary Atlantic milieu that was presented to the likes of Samuel Adams, who encountered their spirit, for example, in the mob actions on the North American colonial seaboard in the 1740s. Especially notable was the 1749 Knowles Riot in Boston. But that riot surfaced atop a wave of other rebellions throughout the 1730s, which were usually orchestrated by slaves. By the time of Adams's meditation on the Knowles Riot, the wave of rebellion had blossomed dramatically, and over a decade's time, in "a multi-ethnic insurrectionary plot by workers in New York City in 1741."[10] In the year 1730 alone, powerful revolts erupted in Virginia, South Carolina, Bermuda, and Louisiana. 1732 featured repeated revolts in Louisiana, followed in 1733 by rebellions in South Carolina, Jamaica, the Danish Virgin Islands, and Dutch Guiana. Somerset, New Jersey had slave uprisings in 1734. Every year of the 1730s featured rebellions somewhere in the colonies.[11] All this was heated up by the long war of Maroons (runaway slaves) in Jamaica, which lasted from about 1728 to 1738. When revolt came to New York City in 1741, beginning on St. Patrick's Day to commemorate Patrick's abolition of slavery in Ireland, a carefully planned rebellion struck at the heart of royal British authority and much of New York. Thirteen fires were set. It was remembered as "the most horrible and destructive plot that was ever yet known in these parts of America."[12] The rebel slaves and rioters in New York had counted on aid from Britain's imperial rival Spain, but it did not materialize, and, as Linebaugh and Rediker make clear, the rioters and their leaders were brutally tortured, pilloried, and hung from posts about the city.

Such stories of rebellion could be multiplied over several volumes. We have cited enough here to see at work a near routinization of revolt, taking place over decades, which prepared the way for the American Revolution in the 1770s and 1780s.

Moreover, to understand the revolutionary tradition to which the American Revolution belongs, prophetic spirit's vision into history would also need to bring to light the pirate cultures of the 1710s and 1720s, which forged a style of rule among these renegade seafarers that historians have termed "hydrarchy," the order of the seas. This shaped habits of collective organization intended to rival the commercial orders of the empire's hierarchically structured ships. When the motley crew from pirate cultures mingled with town crowds, workers, and others, they spread the alternative collective spirit that has rejuvenated the rebellions of the marginalized and repressed time and again.[13]

The motley crew can be traced still further back to the actions of the Diggers and Levellers, those resisting the rising business and trading classes that pushed commoners off publicly shared land in England between 1640 and 1680. Cut adrift and then terrorized by new punishments and repression, many of the Diggers and Levellers resisted, mobilizing older prophetic brews of religion and emancipatory politics to sustain revolt.[14] Even though they lost that struggle to a rising English capitalism, those who went off into colonial exile, to serve on ship or plantation, circulated abroad the English commoners' resistance. The revolutionary mobility, then, was a fluid culture of emigrating and immigrating peoples. If revolutionary belonging is to nurture a revolutionary expectation today in the United States, then its immigrant peoples (Hispanic/Latino/a, Asian, African, European), as I will emphasize below, will also need to play significant roles. During the period of the American Revolution, members of the motley crew mingled at sea and around the Atlantic rim, drawing strength for revolutionary spirit from those many others forced to circulate at sea and in exile. They shared solidarity with those who remembered "the commons" that, in some form, had animated their own and their ancestors' lives. The commons meant "the clachan [town], the sept [clan], the rundale [field], the West African village, and the indigenous tradition of long-fallow agriculture of Native Americans—in other words it encompassed all those parts of the Earth that remained unprivatized, unenclosed, a non-commodity, a support for the manifold human values of mutuality."[15]

Today's American romanticists, as well as the contractual liberals, will often dismiss the rebellions borne in the commons as just so much naïve dreaming, unworthy of remembrance in these times. Prophetic spirit's uncovering of this tradition, though, reminds us that it is today's triumphant romanticists and liberals who commit the greater naïveté, celebrating as they do the discourses of freedom and equality that were, in fact, bequeathed them by the motley crew's centuries of dreaming and fighting to renew the commons. The motley crew as revolutionary subject was driven by this tradition, made possible by these peoples' diverse remembrance of and struggle for the commons.

REVOLUTIONARY MYTHIC LANGUAGE

Revolutionary traditions are energized and strengthened by people through history by their myths, their use of symbols and story to nurture memory and hope. Is there a mythic language for a revolutionary tradition in America that is free from the specter of American romanticism? Are there narratives that, in philosopher William Dean's language, "divine America without divinizing America?"[16] We have taken a first step to divining America, in the sense of discerning America's origins in places behind and beneath received romanticist traditions, all in hope of surfacing a more revolutionary belonging.

This chapter, in fact, might be seen as a kind of divining rod in its attempts to discern a way of belonging that is beneath, or antecedent to, American romanticism. Once that is done and we surface the much repressed revolutionary subject and tradition, we can then discern that this subject and tradition also carry, and are animated by, their own divining languages, their own mythic corpus of symbols and stories.

These languages and mythic elements have come from a variety of religious traditions. To sustain its revolutionary tradition as an active, organizing revolutionary subject, the motley crew has deployed divining and mythic languages as hybrid as its crews have been, motley and multiethnic. It has drawn from the early Hebrew scriptures' accounts of escape from Egypt in Exodus, from stories of the Jubilee year of deliverance of slaves in the book of Leviticus, from Jesus's proclamation of release to the captives in the New Testament Gospels, from John the Baptist's announcement of a time when "the axe would be laid" to the root of Babylon (that is, the king of the powerful), and from numerous other passages in the New Testament that could be used to support counterimperial and economically emancipatory practices.[17] Black preachers and Afro-Christianity merged in sundry and complex syncretisms on several continents, particularly with the cosmologies of indigenous peoples throughout the Americas. The circulation of African culture in the motley crew assumed also that there was a dynamic synergy between all these and Vodou, Obeah, Akan, and Yoruban spirits. If there is to be a mythic language for a revolutionary belonging today, it must take its cue from this motley and multiple mythos. All these traditions and more can be resources for the revolutionary subject. This mythic language gave rise to thought, and entire books might be written on the ideas and beliefs that characterize the revolutionary subject, tradition, and mythic language. These would entail beliefs, for example, like the Leveller notion that "God is no respecter of persons," antinomian ideas that people are not bound to obey laws that violate a higher law of justice, and so on.[18]

Why might a new revolutionary belonging need myth or elements of religious traditions at all? Part of the answer is that it is mythic language, symbols, and traditions, as well as new narratives, that often best express our encounters with the "underivable," with those eruptions of creativity and spirit in human cultural life that have a puzzling, surprising, often wondrous character to them. The liberations dreamed and worked for by the motley crew usually press forward toward goals where no way forward is easily seen. The way forward must always have recourse to a risk of the imagination in order to regenerate revolutionary practice. The revolutionary aims of the motley crew are elusive and almost always remain "not yet." The motley crew, therefore, needs an aesthetics of resistance, an artful dreaming of emancipatory practices and revolutionary fulfillment. Myths, through their legends and stories of past achievements and through their symbols of expectation, are indispensable resources for mobilizing the strength of the motley crew to take on the seemingly impenetrable forces arrayed against it today.

The continual, hybrid mythologizing is a way to build and sustain confidence in face of the mystery in which we ask: How can there be a way forward for the motley crew of diverse humanity toward a liberation held in common? Again, mythic language does not describe that way forward, nor can it supplant the action and the critical thinking required for making that way; but it does vitalize that acting and thinking with the aesthetic powers of imagination. Myth, like most forms of art, is essential to hope. Myth and art make hope for the revolutionary subject and animate revolutionary traditions because they make present aesthetically the "not yet" that they struggle toward. Even if it "only" makes the future present aesthetically, that aesthetic sense is crucial for galvanizing the energy and imagination necessary for practical, material changes toward future liberation.

So it is that the motley crew almost always has reached for a hybrid, motley spiritual discourse. Insofar as we seek a revolutionary belonging in the U.S. today, insofar as we seek to belong to a revolutionary mythic heritage, we would do well to embrace the whole teeming set of spiritualities—from the great religions in the United States (Judaism, Christianity, Islam, Buddhism, and more) in all their variants and subvariants, and also from the no less important (often *more* important) spiritualities of repressed indigenous, Afro-Caribbean, Afro-Christian, Afro-Asian, Latin American traditions, and more. The crucial feature marking these spiritualities is their power to animate the comprehensive program of the revolutionary subject, the world's motley crew and its emancipatory aims.

CONCLUSION:
PROPHETIC SPIRIT,
THE SPECTER OF THE HYDRA

One way to summarize how prophetic spirit can be a specter that resists and transforms the specter of American romanticism in the post-9/11 USA is to deploy another powerful mythic theme, that of the Hydra.

The Hydra in Greek mythology was a many-headed venomous serpent whose heads would grow back whenever cut off; also, when cut into sections, each could regrow into a whole new creature. In Greek mythology, Hercules' second labor was his slaying of the Hydra. He finally did so by sealing off the neck of each head he severed with a lighted torch, and then he used arrows made lethal by the serpent's own poison to finally do it in.

More important than the Greek stories is the way the Hercules-Hydra myth functioned in the history of Western colonialism. It was used repeatedly, from the seventeenth to the nineteenth century "to describe the difficulty of imposing order on increasingly global systems of labor."[19] "Hydra" was the mythic term used by Western commercial and educated elites to symbolize their dread of the multitudinous and resilient forces of workers, which had to be tamed, surveilled, punished, and, depending on the kind of Hydra, exterminated. Francis Bacon, the early seventeenth-century philosopher of induction and scientific reason, also was a philosopher and rationalizer of capitalist and colonial expansion. In those rationalizations, he often deployed the Hercules-Hydra myth, suggesting that capitalists undertake a "labor of Hercules" to achieve the destruction of the enemies of development: "West Indians, Canaanites, pirates, land rovers, assassins, Amazons and Anabaptists."[20] Sir Walter Raleigh, Thomas Hobbes, William Shakespeare, and a host of others deployed the Hydra symbol in this way. Thomas Edwards, a seventeenth-century British writer who sought to catalogue the many heads of heresy as "a Hydra, ready to rise up in their place," took special aim at Levellers, antinomians, and rebels. Edwards styled John Calvin as a "Christian Hercules" because he triumphed over the monstrous papists, Anabaptists, and libertines.[21] John Adams proposed Hercules to be the symbol for the founding fathers' new American nation (while the more motley crew of resisters preferred a banner with the Hydra-like serpent image, with its motto, "Don't Tread on Me.").[22]

Sometimes those reckoned to be the Hydra tried to reverse the symbolism and make of their own motley crew a new Hercules who would subdue the colonizing masters of maritime and plantation economies. More typical, however, was an acceptance by the motley crew of its role as Hydra, then a positive valuing of the Hydra as signal of their liberating power (as in the "Don't Tread on Me" banner). The "hydrarchy" of the pirates' ship community waged vigorous resistance to commercial capitalism until it was crushed by British navies by the 1720s. But its ever multiple, serpentine ways enabled revolution to move mysteriously onward. The Hydra was on the move

> in the multitudes who gathered at the market, in the fields, on the piers and the ships, on the plantations, upon the battlefields. The power of numbers was expanded by movement, as the hydra journeyed and voyaged or was banished or dispersed in diaspora, carried by the winds and waves beyond the boundaries of the nation-state. Sailors, pilots, felons, lovers, translators, musicians, mobile workers of all kinds made new and unexpected connections, which variously appeared to be accidental, contingent, transient, even miraculous.[23]

The way of belonging that marks an alternative to American romanticism's aggressive nationalism helps citizens understand their origin and place within the subjectivity, tradition, and mythic language of the motley crew, always on the move, with a renewal of common life so dangerous to the gentry of every period that it must be called "revolutionary."

In the United States, revolutionary belonging, which is in accord with prophetic spirit's broadening and deepening being, lives in faithfulness to the Hydra. The Hydra's yearning, clamor, resistance, and organizing generate efforts at nation-building but always judging those nations by reference to the desires and needs of an internationally, insurgent motley crew, a greater proletariat, desiring, contesting, and always organizing multitude. In our own time, literature professor Michael Hardt and political philosopher Antonio Negri have proposed, among their many suggestions for resisting empire today, that struggling multitudes own their power as a Hydra—as a monstrous, hybrid, and momentous specter in resistance to imperial power.[24] Prophetic spirit thus is in a relationship of fundamental antagonism with both the Christian Right's American exceptionalist idea of righteous empire and the neoconservatives' version of American Greatness. From the perspective of prophetic spirit, what is "great" about revolutionary belonging is governance that respects and is oriented to the motley crew, to the needs of the Hydra, not to the founding fathers' smaller world. A divinely sanctioned nation-state, with often unilateralist and unipolarist actions of a single nation, embodies more the praxis of the over-celebrated, often elitist cult of Hercules, than peoples' mobile and manifold drives toward freedom as expressed in the Hydra. But how can there be governance and civil structures for the Hydra? Is prophetic spirit's revolutionary belonging to the Hydra a way forward for a mobility that can also govern itself in a meaningful, workable sense? Precisely these questions propel us to the final chapter.

REVOLUTIONARY EXPECTATION

> I want to ask whether in a world of capitalism and states
> a radical liberalism is possible, what it might look like,
> and how it might orient the tasks of political judgment
> and decision at a moment when the political landscape
> has been transformed beyond recognition.
>
> —IRA KATZNELSON, *LIBERALISM'S CROOKED CIRCLE*

Prophetic spirit today does not only offer a new way of revolutionary belonging, a new romance, if you will, that centers us in the mobility of people seeking unity in a complex emancipatory process. That belonging, by its very nature, is also a site of expectation, a desire to move forward, to work release and renewal with the marginalized and oppressed peoples whose emancipation and sustenance are essential for the health of the whole body politic, for the dignity of all public life. Prophetic spirit, then, must indicate what this way forward might be, what revolutionary expectation looks like, thus clarifying what it means today to belong to the traditions I have introduced in the previous chapter.

Amid the play of powers in post-9/11 USA, pointing toward a revolutionary expectation will not be easy. Just as belonging being has been twisted and confined by the 9/11 moment into a resurgent American romanticism, so expectant being has also been twisted by the 9/11 moment, laboring under the confines of a contractual liberalism. Expectant being's rhetorics of freedom, liberty, and democracy are more restricted than ever; the liberalism promised and touted more contractual than ever.

TOWARD A RADICAL LIBERALISM

Contractual liberalism, like most of Western liberalism, has grown strong and perpetuates its contractual and corporatist distortions by twisting citizens' needs for expectant being, their desires to participate in advancement, change, and newness. Contractual liberalism, then, like American romanticism, is a good example of Paul Tillich's notion of "the demonic," a force in life that seizes the vitality of a publicly appealing good, structures them, and then bends them toward destructive ends. "Demonry," says Tillich, "is the form-destroying eruption of the creative basis of things."[1] Today, in the post-9/11 milieu, our creative and basic needs for belonging and expectation are erupting in ways that destroy the forms we need to sustain belonging and expectation for all. The more adequate belonging of prophetic spirit that I proposed in chapter 6 must seek a more adequate expectation that builds hope and less destructive forms than today's consolidating contractual liberalism.

I hasten to note that prophetic spirit does not just counter, stamp out, or repudiate liberalism on the way to more adequate revolutionary expectation. Prophetic spirit resists contractual and corporatist liberalism but takes on the challenge of reconstructing liberalism, or at least reorienting its expectant being within a more complex and radical vision of our social and political landscape. This more complex vision emerges from what I described above as the broadening and deepening being of prophetic spirit. Prophetic spirit's way of being reorients liberal societies' expectant being within a spatial approach that gives texture to history, attending through breadth of vision to the marginalized, through depth of vision to the oppressed and repressed. Such a prophetic reorientation of liberalism yields what Ira Katznelson has called a "textured liberalism," a "liberalism of adjectives" (here, especially, "prophetic"), or, as in the epigraph for this chapter, a "radical liberalism."[2]

Even while sharing Katznelson's drive for such a radical liberalism, I also share his suspicions that the contractual or corporatist restraints on liberal society may be inherent to it, making liberalism unreformable, persisting as a nonrevolutionizable current in history that will always be limited by its contracts in spite of prophetic spirit's impact and influence. It is necessary to admit that liberal society's limitations, its penchant for destructive agendas of class, race, and gender privilege, may never recede enough so that liberalism can stand on its own, surely not without the continual orienting critique of prophetic spirit.

In fact, liberal society has often been parasitic upon radical prophetism, or the broadening and deepening way of being proper to prophetic spirit. Liberalism's discourses of freedom and equality for all, at their best, *depend* on prophetic radicalism.[3] Radical liberalism, then, would involve the rediscovery of liberalism's prophetic roots in, for example, the motley crew of the Atlantic rim during the periods of English and American Revolutions, which prepared the way for the counter-revolutionary liberal project of the U.S. Constitution. Similarly, the liberalisms of John Locke, Immanuel Kant, and Jean-Jacques Rousseau were birthed from a consciousness carried first by revolutionary prophetic movements. Throughout the history of Western liberal societies, the problem is that liberalism's multiple discourses of freedom and equality so often allow themselves to be cut off from their radical, prophetic roots and are thus hemmed in, made subservient to the privileged worlds of contractual and corporatist liberalism. I am thus in agreement with Charles Mills not only when he argues that liberalism is deeply flawed, working with a social contract about civic freedoms underpinned by a racial contract, but also when he argues that liberal society's racial contract is not so much endemic to liberalism or its contract theory but more "a result of the particular conjunctions of circumstances in global history which led to European imperialism."[4] Contractual liberalism, then, amounts to a theft of discourses of freedom by colonizing European elites from the prophetic radical movements of history. Prophetic spirit fights to reclaim those discourses of freedom and to sustain them in a textured space where the needs of people who are marginalized and oppressed are kept to the fore of concerns in a revolutionized liberal society.

Radical Liberalism and "Liberalism"

This search for what I call a "prophetic" or "radical" liberalism thus positions me in what might be called a fourth space among those who interpret liberalism. First, on a more pop-culture level, this book does not occupy the space of those pundits who are the voices so well known in the U.S. media for disparaging liberalism, the Tom DeLays, Ann Coulters, Bill O'Reillys, and others whose rhetoric routinely derides and demonizes "the liberals."[5] There are more sophisticated variations in this space among some realms of theological scholarship, even though scholars here would certainly distance themselves from these media conservatives. Stanley Hauerwas's work, for example, often denounces civic liberalism in preference for practices distinctive to Christian communities.[6] John Milbank's theology, to take another example, positions his preferred "radical orthodoxy" against a secularizing modernity that he traces to "discourses of liberalism."[7] These interpretations tend to see themselves in strong opposition to liberalism.

Second, it is just as true that I am not making any easy defense of liberals, either the popular "blue staters" who passionately vote for the John Kerrys or Bill Clintons, or the liberal scholars who defend, for example, versions of the social contract theory of liberal political philosophies. To the contrary, I think that when we self-identify as belonging to the liberal societies of U.S. party politics, or to the most commonly discussed liberal theories of politics, we risk accommodating public ideals to liberalism's hidden contracts, i.e., to its white racism, its sexism, its violence toward gay and lesbian communities, its exploitative capitalism, and its U.S. nationalism. As I pointed out above, neoconservatives' nationalism and allegiances to American Greatness can be found in the ranks of blue-state "liberal" worlds of Democratic Party politics as well as in Republican strongholds of the U.S. heartland. Some of the red-state demonizing of blue-state liberals (as latté-slurping East coasters, for example) is a populist defense mechanism by people in other parts of the country who, as Thomas Frank and Anatol Lieven point out, fight against an often class-based liberal disdain toward them.[8] For this reason, as well as because of the often more serious hidden contracts carried by liberal society, my pursuit of a radical liberalism should not be mistaken as a defense of this kind of liberalism, even though I retain use of the term "liberalism."

The radical liberalism of this book may be closer to a third site at which liberalism has been interpreted, that of an Emersonian/Whitmanesque tradition of liberal democratic society, as Jeffrey Stout has presented this in his book, *Democracy and Tradition*. Stout is clearly critical of the hidden contracts of liberalism and takes aim at the distortions of racism, gender injustice, politics by managerial elites, curtailment of citizen liberties in post-9/11 USA, and so on. The prophetic spirit of radical liberalism in this book, however, seems to occupy a fourth space, one that can be differentiated from Stout's anti-traditional Emersonian democratic vision, because it seeks to radicalize liberalism further. This book radicalizes liberalism by explicitly foregrounding the agency of marginalized and oppressed groups in public life as the primary collective forces of transformation. Prophetic spirit's radical liberalism reminds all seeking to cultivate expectant being in liberal society that the virtues of that society are lost without the spatial consciousness that turns continually, and gives strategic priority, to the multiple and ever-changing sites of people who suffer *and* resist at the margins and on the undersides of history. That consciousness, when brought to liberalism, radicalizes it. That consciousness preserves liberalism without defending or continuing the hegemony of contractual liberalism. That consciousness of prophetic spirit is what situates this book in a fourth space among interpretations of liberalism.

The two central questions of a radical liberalism that intertwine throughout the rest of this chapter are these: (1) Who are the historical bearers of a prophetic spirit today who might help break the contracts of contractual liberalism and by doing so begin to foment and foster revolutionary expectation in the post-9/11 USA? and (2) In what ways can these bearers of prophetic spirit undertake this work? To ask such questions is to move from the motley crew as revolutionary subject with its revolutionary

tradition and myth, to the governance by which fulfilled promises of revolutionary change might be expected. If liberalism is
about extending liberty and equality to all, it is appropriate that
it reflects on governance, the conducting of policy and affairs of a
people for distributing and orchestrating liberty and equality for
all. Given that the U.S. still faces contractual liberalism as one of
the virulent specters in the post-9/11 USA, what would a radical
liberalism of prophetic spirit look like?

Without offering a blueprint, let me here draw out certain
implications of prophetic spirit in order to identify the main concerns of a post-9/11 radical liberalism. Prophetic spirit's revolutionary expectation issues in a radical liberalism that can be
sketched in terms of (a) its agents, (b) its genres, and (c) its distinctive social practices.

AGENTS OF REVOLUTIONARY EXPECTATION

Prophetic spirit's agents for expressing and embodying expectant
being, for forging a radical liberalism, will come from the leadership of the marginalized and oppressed and those in authentic
solidarity with them. Many of these are today severely alienated,
and often excluded, from present systems of governance, and yet
they are also engaged in diverse modes of resistance. Prophetic
spirit poses the specter of those leaders and groups taking their
places as key catalysts and decision makers for future governance.
I emphasize that in the examples given in this section I am speaking of both groups *and* individuals. Although prophetic spirit
is a historical-cultural tradition and hence most distinguished
for its social or collective character—which it must be to deal
with the collective currents it struggles with—prophetic spirit
also engages individual action and galvanizes personal exercises
of freedom and action. To speak of prophetic spirit's "agents"
of revolutionary expectation is to speak of both individuals and
groups.

The lament, rage, and organizing work of marginalized and
oppressed people today are continuations of that revolutionary

tradition, and of that revolutionary subject whose mobility against the powerful in the motley crew has such a long history. Today's protestors and radicals, in resistance to various oppressions, are not new phenomena. They are bearers of our most revolutionary pasts. My list of them here is by no means exhaustive, but I want to provide sufficient diversity in it to show that a revolutionary expectation might be emergent from many sectors of post-9/11 U.S. society.

There are surely different ways of listing and organizing the eleven important groups I identify below as agents of revolutionary expectation. The criteria operative for my highlighting of these are three. First, each group has representative leaders who have articulated their commitment to elements of the revolutionary subject and tradition that I summarized in chapter 6. Second, these groups and their leaders exemplify or seek to exemplify the qualities of the broadening and deepening way of being that I argued is the hallmark of prophetic spirit. Third, each of these groups shows signs of and special potential for manifesting the genres and social practices of revolutionary expectation that I present in the concluding two sections of this chapter.

Readers will note that I have not listed among these agents any churches or other religious communions. This is because I have already commented throughout this text on the various relations of religious communities to prophetic spirit. Christian and other religious agents and groups can find their way into any and all of the following groups, especially if those groups take seriously the prophetic traditions of their respective faiths, or somehow interpret their symbols, beliefs, and doctrines in ways that accord with prophetic spirit. Prophetic spirit, as developed in this book, is a public, social practice more encompassing than any religious tradition. Nevertheless, as a member of one of the traditions that has a strong prophetic strand, Christianity, I hope that Christians and other religious faithful will find their ways into the larger human struggle that is at work in the social practices of prophetic spirit. Let us turn now to the eleven agents of revolutionary expectation that I highlight here.

DISSENTING U.S. MILITARY VETERANS AND THEIR SUPPORTIVE FAMILIES

The dissent of this group may take various forms, from filing for conscientious objector status, to resisting call-up orders to report for duty in Iraq or elsewhere, to outright flight from the country to avoid service. There are often different reasons for these dissenting actions, ranging from a personal sense that one has already done one's duty for a sufficient time and shouldn't be pressed to do more, to military families' perceptions that U.S. armed forces are being unwisely led or inattentive to needs of military personnel, or to strong personal convictions that current U.S. military adventures, especially in Iraq since March 2003, are in themselves unwise, unjust violations of international law and human dignity. All of these forms and rationales for dissent (and more) can be found in dissenting military groups like Iraq Veterans Against the War.[9] Again, it is not the mere fact of dissent that makes these military veterans, often with their families' support, to be agents of revolutionary expectation; it is their manifestation of broadening and deepening being, whereby they often identify with the needs of citizens in the countries attacked by U.S. forces and also with the deep traditions of revolutionary mobility and democracy in U.S. history.

Those refusing service in the U.S. military regime today might be seen as roughly analogous to the many sailors and port citizens of the past who resisted impressments into imperial navies and so helped build the revolutionary ferment of the motley crew that was the driving force of the American Revolution. Whether inside or outside the ranks of the military today, prophetic spirit is carried by those dissenting from the military onslaught of the U.S. imperial adventuring that is grounded in unilaterally exercised military might.

FAMILIES AND ADVOCATES FOR THE 2.1 MILLION PEOPLE NOW IMPRISONED IN THE UNITED STATES

In the last two decades of the twentieth century, the U.S. prison population quadrupled in size, entailing a prison-building project that has been described as "the largest, most frenetic correctional build up in the history of world cultures."[10] Over 70 percent of people incarcerated in the U.S. are people of color; nearly a full 50 percent are African American.[11]

Many of the confined people are being broken of mind, will, and spirit while serving out their long sentences, often in harsh conditions of solitary confinement in segregated housing units and supermaximum prisons. They often die early with poor health care, exposed to inmate and official violence. Nevertheless, from these ranks savvy organizations for a revolutionary perspective are also emerging. Writings by those in prison, such as Mumia Abu-Jamal, Paul Wright, Reggie Lewis, and many others, are coming from those who have survived some of the worst that the imperial specter can do to the human spirit. They also have seen up close the way human beings can be brutalized and broken by the bureaucratized violence of confinement but also how human beings can resist and break free from the brutal prison ethos. "In time, flesh will wear out chains," writes Abu-Jamal from Pennsylvania's death row, quoting Russian dissident and novelist Victor Serge. Many of these qualify as political prisoners in the United States, and they carry an especially savvy and tough discernment about the ways of power.[12] The revolutionary future will need the expertise of agents who know how flesh needs to work when up against a system's chains, how flesh might work on overcoming when up against such odds.[13]

ACTIVISTS AND LEADERS IN U.S.-BASED BLACK REPARATIONS MOVEMENTS

White racism will continue to take its toll on generations of U.S. citizens—not just on African Americans but on all ethnic groups—until a qualitatively new restorative act toward the descendents of chattel slavery in the U.S. is legally enacted.

As historian Robin D. G. Kelley has pointed out, there is an abundance of different kinds of judicious reparations proposals in circulation today.[14] These have gained strength from legal and financial reparations (often still inadequate) that have been made to Japanese Americans who suffered in U.S. internment camps during World War II; to Alaskan indigenous peoples who lost land and control of natural resources in their territories; to black communities in Rosewood, Florida, who suffered loss of property from white mob violence in the 1920s; and some Jewish families of Holocaust victims whose reparations have come from German governments. Michigan congressman John Conyers has kept a reparations bill for black people in Congress since 1989. In contemporary groups like the National Coalition of Blacks for Reparations in America and the Black Radical Congress, the reparations proposals being made "focus less on individual payments than on securing funds to build autonomous black institutions, improving community life, and in some cases establishing a homeland that will enable African Americans to develop a political economy geared toward collective needs than toward [individual] accumulation."[15] For these reparations movements to come to fruition for African Americans (or for any other groups such as Latino/a or various Asian communities, whose properties have been systematically targeted in various ways), for prophetic spirit to work any real revolutionary expectation in a persistently racist America—with its white overclass and especially brutal imperial movements against the world's people of color—leaders of these reparations movements in the U.S., and their proposals, need to be given a central role.

ACTIVISTS AND MOVEMENTS AMONG
SOCIALLY DISPOSSESSED PEOPLE

Here are those in resistance to our society's racial contract fighting the many forms of racial discrimination. Here, too, are those women's movements challenging the sexual contract of the U.S. order in a host of grassroots movements. Movements among people with disabilities, who fight their neglect by society and their vulnerability to impoverishment and inadequate medical care, are crucial catalysts of prophetic spirit. Labor unions and groups struggling for workers' rights and a "living wage" are key agents of revolutionary expectation. These, along with other groups, challenge the draconian ways of the U.S. economic elite. Activists also work on behalf of people without health care, without employment and housing and, perhaps soon, with much reduced Social Security benefits and inadequate Medicare provisions. Organizations of retirees and senior citizens, who face the challenges of aging with dignity or devising long-term care options, also display a perspective on the entire social order that is important to hear. The MOVE organization in Philadelphia has given crucial support to displaced urban people and supports national movements for political prisoners.[16] All these make up a restless, organizing mobility from which new action emerges.

Exemplary movements and groups could be many. Perhaps especially exemplary of these movements among socially dispossessed people is the Kensington Welfare Rights Union in Philadelphia under the leadership team catalyzed by activist Cheri Honkala.[17] With a strong presence of women from diverse ethnic and age groups, this organization addresses simultaneously the social distortions worked by the sexual, racial, and economic contracts that so often make a joke of liberal rhetorics of freedom and progress.

IMMIGRANTS SEEKING JUSTICE

Since 9/11, Arab and South Asian immigrants especially have faced new levels of discrimination, persecution, and outright imprisonment, often without any information given as to why they are so mistreated or confined. Xenophobia practiced toward immigrants fosters a host of new abusive practices, of judicial and extrajudicial actions against immigrants. Even before 9/11, however, immigrants were targeted with large-scale racial persecution, often segregated for social ills even as they were exploited to do work that U.S. citizens were reluctant to do.

Advocacy movements for immigrants emergent before 9/11, largely along the U.S.-Mexican border, are crucial sources of revolutionary agency, as are post-9/11 groups such as the Coalition for the Human Rights of Immigrants and the National Network for Immigrant and Refugee Rights.[18] Agents from the cultures of immigrant advocacy in the U.S. add a crucial internationalist perspective to revolutionary liberal discourse inside the U.S. Immigrants' often debilitating confinement to borderland regions of U.S. culture make them a key contributor to a revolutionary future in which national boundaries will have to be re-constituted, if not renegotiated or re-drawn, to allow a more humane and just movement of peoples and workers across them. At present, maximum flexibility of travel across borders is afforded to owners of capital and means of production, while a minimum of flexibility is extended to those who only have their labor to sell. In sum, the movement of immigrants—vulnerable, on the run, always shifting, traversing boundaries—is crucial for crafting governance out of revolutionary liberalism. The U.S.-Mexican border, in particular, is what Chicana intellectual, poet, and activist Gloria Anzaldúa has called "*una herida abierta* [an open wound] where the Third World grates against the first and bleeds. And before a scab forms it hemorrhages again, the lifeblood of two worlds merging to form a third country—a border culture." Border desert areas have become "fields of death" for restless, poor immigrants caught up in the flow of labor from South to North in globalization's many streams.[19] But from the border wounds, there is the new vision of "border thinking,"[20] and new resources for binding up the larger wounded body politic that is the USA. Immigrants in the U.S.— whether from Africa, Latin America, Asia, or Europe—can be a crucial resource for a mobility dangerous to established gentries. During the second administration of George W. Bush, media and public scapegoating of immigrants in the U.S.-Mexico border areas for wider problems of unemployment, for example, tends to overrun serious reflection on the contributions that immigrants make to U.S. society and the exploitation they suffer in the process. Acknowledging the agency of immigrant leaders and labor groups can help forge a more humane immigration policy and enhance the entire society.

Pressing as they surely will for a more fluid sense of borders, immigrants from Mexico, Central, and South America will especially equip a revolutionary future to remember that being "American" means to belong to and work with all those of "the

Américas." I write here of América/Américas with the Span-
ish language accent mark to signal the fullness of peoples who
in North, Central, and South America rightly claim the name
"American." Moreover, they may choose to invoke precoloniza-
tion titles for their continents, drawing from their own heritages
(for example, "Great Island," "Turtle Island," "Abya Yala"[21]). Such
peoples, inside and outside the United States, help to dream and
achieve a usage of the moniker "American" so that it no longer
refers only to U.S. citizens, whose leaders have so long insisted on
maintaining privileged control over the hemisphere and policing
their nation's borders to keep out, or keep control over, the many
to the south.[22]

LEADERS OF INDIGENOUS PEOPLES AND
NATIONS OF THE AMERICAS

This group is one of the most important redressive forces for
any revolutionary expectation in the United States. Native
Americans, along with others in the history of the revolutionary Atlantic, played a crucial role in forming the revolutionary
subject, the motley crew. Even though their numbers have been
decimated in the United States by centuries of forced removal,
massacre, and often deliberately spread disease, they are still a
vigorous presence in the United States. Although they make up
only about 1 percent of the population, indigenous groups in the
U.S. have nurtured some shared vision and purpose by building global connections with indigenous networks, as with the
Maya movement of Guatemala and Mexico, and with indigenous
movements worldwide.[23] Since the nation's founding, U.S. governments have officially ratified and then violated hundreds of
treaties with indigenous peoples. The land of the U.S. would not
be available without the forced expropriation of indigenous territories.[24] Indigenous agents of revolutionary expectation bring
a memory of that global move of Western colonizing modernity
against indigenous societies, a memory that will entail negotiat-
ing their legitimate claims for land restoration and reparations
in ways that meet their peoples' ongoing needs. They also bring

a legacy of careful consideration and respect for the carrying capacity of the land vis-à-vis human populations. This knowledge has been proven indispensable for all who would inhabit North American lands, and not just to the special concerns of indigenous peoples. Not only do indigenous peoples suffer especially high rates of poverty in the U.S. today and bear a long list of other grievances that need to be redressed in any revolutionary governance, they also bring distinctive perspectives that will be necessary for shaping a revolutionary future on the North American mainland.[25]

ENVIRONMENTAL ACTIVIST GROUPS

Groups that monitor not only the carrying capacity of the populace's land-base, but also the quality of air, water, flora and fauna and the threats to their flourishing, will also be necessary as contributing agents of a radical pluralism. A revolutionary future that does not protect the rights of species—animals and plants— within the protective balance of our ecostructure cannot be a truly revolutionary one. At present, the specters of American romanticism and contractual liberalism have yielded a national project with imperial designs and policies at home and abroad that place the earth's climate and ecology at risk. Prophetic spirit's revolutionary expectation for human flourishing must seek to be attuned to the rhythms of nature even as it seeks justice and fairness for different social groups.[26]

ADVOCATES AND PRACTITIONERS OF CITIZENS' NECESSARY SEXUAL FREEDOMS

What people do with their bodies, especially regarding the health and pleasure of their sexuality, often affects whether and how they embrace change politically. It is no accident, therefore, that the post-9/11 imperial regime in the U.S. has entailed also a moralistic colonization of peoples' lives by the Christian Right, especially by promoting such policies as doctrinaire sexual abstinence programs for youth and heterosexual-only marriage laws for family life. Voices who work as agents of prophetic spirit would challenge this dimension of imperial American culture.

Prophetic spirit need not deploy some left-wing countermoralism against sexual abstinence or against heterosexual marriage, but it does give open place to those whose sexual lives have long been marginalized and repressed and whose needs therefore need to be rethought in a comprehensive prophetic revisioning.

Such agents would include leaders at work in (a) women's organizations fighting for full and open reproductive health and abortion counseling, and for the freedom to choose abortion in that matrix of counseling; (b) groups pressing for marriage rights for same-sex couples; (c) movements that seek more open and supportive policies for all couples (regardless of their sexual or gender identities) who wish to live together without being married; (d) organizations pressing for the legalization of sex work and prostitution when providers today remain especially vulnerable to abuse and exploitation because their work is illegal, hidden, and shamed; (e) societies of consenting adults entertaining forms of sexual bondage-and-submission lifestyles as a way to heal from abuses of power, or to enhance mutual empowerment and pleasure;[27] and (f) agencies offering more open and direct modes of sex education, at home and in public life, for the youth of society.

To be sure, these are all controversial proposals, and the groups working toward these ends meet with vigorous opposition from many in the present context of "culture wars" in U.S. society. The debates on the moral dimensions of sexual practice and freedom are intense. Work will have to progress on these matters, then, not simply through advocacy and protest, but especially through deliberative reasoning, one of the key genres of revolutionary expectation that I will discuss in the next section of this chapter.

Immigrant persons from other countries and cultural traditions can often play a mitigating role in the overheated discussions about these issues in the United States. They might point to a wider variety of cultural options for facilitating the practice of a fuller sexual freedom in American societies without resorting to what many fear as a path to unprincipled sexual chaos. The work here will not be easy, but the decolonization of American sexual bodies is an important dimension of prophetic spirit.

SOCIALIST GROUPS AND THEIR LEADERS

These activists represent the often beleaguered but occasionally strong legacy of socialist and communist movements in the U.S., and they must also find their place among the agents of revolutionary expectation.[28] They have developed some of the most trenchant and informed criticisms of world capitalist systems and of capitalist structures in the United States. Moreover, in the post-9/11 USA, the large mobilizations of citizens against the war in Iraq and for immigrant rights and protection have often been due to the agitation and work of groups advocating for a socialist future. The work of the International Action Center, associated with Workers World, is noteworthy in this regard because it played such key roles in the mass mobilizations against the U.S. wars and racism in Afghanistan and Iraq in 2002 and 2003.

To the extent that such groups are open to wide-ranging debate with the many other groups that make up a revolutionary future, socialist theorists and organizers are key agents, and they bring important organizing skills.[29] Socialist thought and organizing should not be dismissed by prophetic spirit as mere vanguardist posturing; rather, socialist resources are crucial for understanding and mobilizing broad sectors of humanity that seek new revolutionary communities of justice, peace, and equality. Prophetic spirit works a socialist future within a vision shaped by the multitude[30]—the greater proletariat of proactive, multicultural organizing by marginalized and oppressed movements of all kinds—and socialist agents play an essential role in that emergent multitude. Prophetic spirit's revolutionary expectation may issue in forms of revolutionary change that depart from socialist forms, but prophetic spirit cannot ignore socialism's own revolutionary heritage and vision.

STUDENTS AND CERTAIN YOUTH MOVEMENTS

Youth who practice prophetic spirit often work with a striking sense of new possibility, the energies of young people, and a willingness to risk new strategies. Without overlooking the key roles of more experienced citizens, we can nevertheless observe that youth's energy and organizing frequently bring important vigor to people's movements and so can build revolutionary expectation. Youth and student courage, resolve, and energy animated many of the groups, religious and secular, that helped build the Civil Rights Movement of the 1950s and 1960s.[31] Among youth of color in the United States today, for another example, musical traditions such as rap and hip hop have made crucial contributions to identifying marginalization and repression and to resisting them.[32] Youth strategies of organizing, acting up, and deploying theater and miming in the streets have reinvigorated several parts of movement culture, especially the alternative globalization movements developing since the Seattle protests against the World Trade Organization in 1999.[33] Students on U.S. college and university campuses have also had a notable impact in campaigns against sweatshops run by corporate giants.[34]

INTERNATIONAL CITIZEN MOVEMENTS
OUTSIDE THE UNITED STATES

In this era of U.S. hegemony, the world's peoples are increasingly stakeholders in the policies drafted by the United States of America. While some planners of U.S. policy seek what they call "full-spectrum dominance" and declare the next hundred years to be "the American century," the vast majority of the world's population is denied representation and, of course, cannot vote to influence U.S. leadership. These citizens of the world have a key role to play, however, in crafting and sustaining revolutionary expectation.

A revolutionary future of prophetic spirit will seek ways to make international citizenry co-present with U.S. residents in drafting radical liberalism's vision and form of governance.[35] International and transnational elites in Europe and Asia, in particular, can make decisions that often affect economic developments and political movements internal to the United States because of their influence on financial markets that affect the U.S. economy.[36] Other countries, too, especially those that make crucial contributions to oil and natural gas supply, such as Venezuela and Nigeria, have key roles. A radical liberalism will invite such powerful decision makers abroad not to leave U.S. hegemony unchallenged and unprotested. International citizen movements—whether from grassroots movements or from new leaders of less powerful but significant countries such as Hugo Chavez in Venezuela, Luiz Inácio Lula da Silva in Brazil, or others—must do what they can to interrupt and disrupt the military and economic programs that U.S. unilateralist projects have designed to underwrite the superpower status of the United States. Movements of revolutionary expectation in the United States will need to take up common cause and forge links with agents in those international movements.

Before examining what kinds of actions or practices agents like these might take up, I turn in the next section to certain genres of revolutionary expectation.

GENRES OF REVOLUTIONARY EXPECTATION

By turning to genres, I am viewing the process of nurturing revolutionary expectation as a kind of art—an art involving certain styles, or genres. The many cries and claims of aforementioned agents of revolutionary expectation cannot proceed directly to policy proposal and practice. It is foolish to expect so. Given what revolutionary expectation is up against, that is, organized powers whose discourses of freedom are cruelly restricted by their relentless allegiance to discriminatory contracts and their frequent use of brutal repression—given all this, seekers of a prophetic revolutionary expectation, of a truly radical liberalism, must usually deploy more indirect forms. The following three genres should all be seen as necessary, intertwining with one another as strands for the strengthening of revolutionary expectation toward practice of a radical liberalism. The revolutionary "agents," which I identified in the previous section, are further distinguished by their willingness and ability to deploy these genres.

Aesthetic Imagination

This first genre, perhaps the most important, is a starting place for revolutionary expectation and a sustaining power for it. If nurturing revolutionary expectation is an art, it begins with aesthetic imagination. Radical change is birthed from those who survive and dream through poetry, story, novel, painting (including murals and graffiti), sculpture, and especially music. Within conditions of oppression, these art forms not only are expressions of joy, admiration and pleasure, but also are often essential for forging grief and rage into a focused and transforming lament. In these ways, the arts in movements for social change help make hope because they allow people in the present to taste what they dream, which often remains achingly postponed to a future time. Through the aesthetic imagination, agents of revolutionary expectation keep alive the mythic symbols of revolutionary belonging, which we discussed in the previous chapter. Aesthetically tasting the hoped-for future galvanizes work in the present that is needed to move toward the imagined future. What Kelley writes about surrealist art we may generally say about a revolutionary aesthetic: "By plunging into the depths of the unconscious and lessening 'the contradiction between everyday life and our wildest dreams,' we can enter or realize the domain of the Marvelous."[37]

The revolutionary subject and tradition that carry prophetic spirit and the revolutionary expectation that prophetic spirit nurtures depend upon this hope-making imagery of expectation. This imagery need not always be religious; in fact often it is not. But because myth and symbol, forms of art and imagination, have been the ordinary and most powerful discourses of religious communities, the religious imagination has often been involved in nurturing revolutionary expectation. The black freedom struggle especially brought music, not only spirituals but also the blues. This made up a veritable "aesthetics of resistance" that philoso-

pher and activist Angela Y. Davis has explored in her studies of
Gertrude "Ma" Rainey Harper, Bessie Smith, and Billie Holiday.[38]
These, and others like Sippie Wallace, John Lee Hooker, and Joe
Louis Walker, worked this resistance through a blues aesthetic,
which, as Ralph Ellison so well described it, is "an impulse to
keep the painful details and episodes of a brutal experience alive
in one's aching consciousness, to finger its jagged grain, and to
transcend it, not by the consolation of philosophy but by squeezing
from it a near-tragic, near-comic lyricism."[39] Then, too, within
this tradition of blues lamentation, there is the equally necessary
earthy, apocalyptic aggressiveness in the steady drum and dance-
able rhythms of what poet and English professor Kwame Dawes
terms "the Reggae aesthetic," its revolutionary power embodied
so powerfully in the music of Bob Marley.[40]

Almost all freedom struggles tap into some musical roots. For
example, there are the mountain musics of Appalachian miners,
and the ballads of Woody Guthrie, Bob Dylan, and Bruce Springsteen that have given voice to the American artistic visions of
Walt Whitman and often give voice to those left behind.[41] U2 of
Ireland, the Asian-Dub Foundation emergent from Asian American traditions, KRS1 and Dead Presidents from the urban USA,
Bright Eyes out of the U.S. Midwest, Ozomatli and Ricanstruc-
tion from U.S. Latino/a syncretic culture, Nigeria's Fela Kuti,
South Africa's Mzwaki Mbuli and Lucky Dube, Zaire's Thomas
Mapfumo, China's Cui Jian of the Tiananmen Square movement
years—these are just a few examples of contemporary artists who
dream artfully and sustain revolutionary expectation.

Most of the agents and movements mentioned in the previous section organize out of artistic and imaginative resources.
Many military dissenters today rally to the sounds of Phil Ochs
(still), Billy Bragg, and Bruce Springsteen; many prison inmates
have turned out volumes of poetry and painting; the socially dispossessed of many stripes have tuned up their organizing to the
sounds of reggae, hip hop, folk, funk, and fusion.

The radical liberalism of prophetic spirit will be stillborn if
it does not lead with the genre of aesthetic imagination. Indeed,
so central is art to expectation that there is no prophetic spirit

without it. It is of the essence of prophetic spirit, if and when it is present, to catalyze its movement with art, the imaginative dreaming that brings the cries of the oppressed into a focused lament, making possible a way forward.

PUBLIC ENACTMENT

A second genre arises from aesthetic imagination. It is the public enactment of artful expectation in the streets and at meeting places frequented by many citizens. Marching, street action, activists' protests, street theater, and "makin' noise" are means for agents and movements of revolutionary expectation to build support for their revolutionary dreams. Artists and advocates have to make change by acting out and acting up in public, with raised voice, clamor, and demands. It has always been so with the revolutionary subject, with the Atlantic traditions of the motley crew, and it remains doubtful whether prophetic spirit's creation of a radical liberalism can do without it.

Part of the "motliness" of the motley crew was its unruliness, its moving into public spaces to interrupt normal flows, to display people's suffering, to point to alternative policies. In the colonial North America of the 1770s, for example, it was often the clamorous outbursts and impromptu organizing of activists that put citizens in the streets, organized petition drives, and so helped defeat many of the British king's oppressive rulings, even before an official militia was formed. Residents of the American colonies intimidated the king's representatives with mob threats, confronted royal personnel in public, even filled up courtrooms so as to bring the British judiciary to a standstill in parts of Massachusetts.[42] Revolutionary expectation will not be nurtured, a truly radical pluralism will not come to pass, without these public enactments of expectation.

One can see this revolutionary motliness alive today. In the United States, antiwar activists clogged major cities on the eve of the 2003 U.S. attack on Iraq. Many less notable pilgrimages, walks, and marches of protest were performed in neighborhoods throughout the country. Thousands have gone each November for the last several years to gather at the U.S. Army School at Fort Benning, Georgia, seeking closure of that military institution, which for years has taught techniques of torture and repression to Latin American military personnel.[43] On other fronts, opponents to the present globalized economic order have taken street theater to new levels in major cities of the U.S., such as Seattle, Washington, DC, and New York, and then to metropolitan areas abroad as well.

After 9/11, security and surveillance have tightened everywhere, raising the quotient of fear for activists who dare to act out their criticism in public spaces. It is especially amid the present government's surveillance culture, however, that the Atlantic revolutionary tradition of the motley crew and its clamor need to be practiced. To be quiescent, to leave public spaces to a tranquility created by overseers, is to lose the chance prophetic spirit needs to engage those who might enliven radical pluralism. As human and civil liberties are spurned, as torture from U.S. precinct stations to Abu Ghraib become known, curtailments against civil liberties must be publicly exposed, and the public must be organized to display its revulsion in as dramatic a way as possible. What patriots dared to do in order to open up the American Revolution in the 1770s we need to do today, seeking equivalents to their closing of courts and their forcing of official resignations by government leaders on the eve of American revolution. This was part of a prior revolutionary period that occurred before the outbreak of hostilities that U.S. textbooks today call the "Revolutionary War." This was a period when, for example, "thousands upon thousands of farmers and artisans seized power from every Crown-appointed official in Massachusetts outside of Boston," and multi-county actions that targeted British courts for closing were a crucial part of this revolutionary period.[44]

DELIBERATIVE REASONING

This third crucial genre, deliberative reasoning, though very different from the public enactments with their motley clamor, is not incompatible with those actions. Simply to negotiate the nature and limits of mob action, as was done in the time of Massachusetts citizens' fomenting of revolution in the 1770s, is to show some important deliberative restraint amid unruly actions of protest. "Even the nighttime mobs (and there were many) maintained a democratic aspect," writes U.S. historian Ray Raphael about Massachusetts crowd actions of 1774. One mob, as witnessed by Abigail Adams, cut short a successful action against a local sheriff to take a vote on whether the crowd should also "disturb the Sabbath." They voted not to do so.[45] This crowd's debate about its actions, its vote, and then the group's abiding by the vote constitute part of its democratic aspect. It is what separates the revolutionary mob from a thuggish gang that only rampages and vents. It is a display of self-criticism, of seeking perspective from others, of discussing motivations and objectives together, of exchanging reasons with one another about actions taken, of being deliberative.

Deliberative reasoning does not operate only in crowd protest actions. Even more important will be its role in the negotiations that must go on between the various agents of revolutionary expectation, which I delineated in the previous section. Since their diverse interests often cut against each other, deliberative reasoning will have to become a revolutionary public virtue. As Jeffrey Stout says so well in *Democracy and Tradition,* the discursive habit or practice of "holding one another responsible for the actions we commit, the commitments we undertake, and the sort of people we become" is the "central and definitive component" of cultures of democratic community.[46] This cultural habit, what I am calling "deliberation and civic reasoning," is crucial for nurturing any successful revolutionary expectation. It is the third strand among the genres of revolutionary expectation, especially as prophetic spirit nurtures that expectation toward actual practice of its radical liberalism.

Prophetic spirit breaks the power of gentrified elites of all types, especially their contractual liberalism, by means of a revolutionary expectation that weaves together the genres of aesthetic imagination, public enactment, and deliberative civic reasoning. These will not be easily held together. There are qualities of each that do not easily abide qualities of the others. An aesthetics of resistance that creatively projects future freedoms onto a screen for dramatic action, for example, will not always adapt easily to the mutual criticism of deliberative civic reasoning. Deliberative reasoners, on the other hand, may not be disposed to march in the streets to enact publicly their visions of the future. Prophetic spirit, though, works to create spaces wherein practitioners of all three genres learn to respect their need for one another. The future of a radical expectation depends upon their mutual interplay. Artists' dreams, public clamor and performance, and deliberative reasoning must coalesce for a radical liberalism to be born.

PRACTICES OF REVOLUTIONARY EXPECTATION

The three genres sketched above might be taken as the practices sufficient for revolutionary expectation. They are, however, more the essential styles, the prefiguring practices that open toward a more organized set of planning practices. It is the purpose of this final section to suggest what might be the particular practices needed in the post-9/11 USA, as its residents struggle under conditions of American political romanticism, contractual liberalism, and their strong alliances with one another today, forging a regime of power with ever-stronger imperial designs and managerial elitism. I hasten to underscore that what I offer in this final section is far from being a blueprint for action, surely not an exhaustive delineation of a program. The proposal here will need criticism from several vantage points, but the kind of proposal I make here is a way to exemplify the discourse necessary for planning practices that are consonant with prophetic spirit's critical engagement and transformation of American romanticism and contractual liberalism. Prophetic spirit's revolutionary expectation requires planning practices as well as identifying revolutionary agents and embracing revolutionary genres.

The focus of my proposal centers around a call for what I term a form of movement conciliarism, public efforts to form paragovernment councils in which the agents mentioned above and their supporters, using the genres of revolutionary expectation, seek to plan practices of radical liberalism in post-9/11 United States of America. The ways of organizing these councils could vary, by particular public interests, by the distinctive identities of groups, by clustering the many movements for change that are already at work today, or by noting their different geographical regions. Whatever the mode and principle of selecting these councils may be, the important point is to begin organizing these paragovernment councils to further the organized strength of marginalized and oppressed communities within the regime of power we confront today.

What is meant by designating these councils as "paragovernmental?" The basic idea is that they are beyond and distinct from, although analogous to, the present U.S. federal government. Since the present U.S. government is swiftly moving its powers of control beyond any meaningful accountability to the masses of ordinary citizens, citizens must begin to form their own alternative structures in an organized way, even if for some time to come these have a largely symbolic character, not really rivaling the power of formal forms of governance. These councils may have something of the character of the "shadow presidential nominating conventions," which U.S. activists organized in 2004 for the purpose of displaying prominently the broader concerns citizens wanted to see aired in a presidential campaign but were being ignored by the Republican and Democratic parties. These had, as would the councils I discuss here, a largely performative or dramatic character, but they also put in motion real changes in the organizing habits of the citizenry. Participants in such a conciliarism could, and probably should, still participate in existing government structures, pressing the interests of prophetic spirit and its agents there, in every way they still can. But the work of organizing people along the lines of some paragovernment conciliarism needs also to be formalized as much as possible to compensate for the limits and failures of standing governments, and to ready a citizenry for alternative forms of democratic practice.

Paragovernment councils, even though they only "shadow" government structures, begin to organize an alternative mode for expressing popular sovereignty. They help prevent the atomization of the citizenry and its subordination to the growing power and incursions of the state. Prophetic spirit's radical liberalism seeks to organize and embody a counterpower through such councils, using the agency and genres of revolutionary expectation among marginalized and oppressed groups.

It may be objected that the formation of citizen councils in the U.S. has a sinister history with respect to the nation's history of governance. Obviously, some citizen councils have a notorious, racist past, as with the white citizen councils that formed to support and enforce Jim and Jane Crow policies across the south.[47] These, though, as should be clear from the claims and arguments of chapters 5, 6, and 7 in this book, are hardly manifestations of prophetic spirit's revolutionary belonging and expectation, even if they style themselves as in resistance to some features of U.S. government. The task of prophetic spirit's movement conciliarism is to hold U.S. governing structures accountable to the highest standards of governance, as these are negotiated by and among the diverse agents of revolutionary expectation. The white racism and other distortions (elitism, class bias, patriarchal deformations, etc.) that have characterized other conciliarist efforts in the U.S. past are examples of precisely what is criticized by prophetic spirit's movement conciliarism.

As these paragovernment councils of prophetic spirit tap and nurture their aesthetic imagination, as they organize mass mobilizations to publicly enact and plead their cases with the wider public, *and* as they season both their art and public enactment with deliberative reasoning, they may challenge and provoke the standing federal government to enact and embody the programs of the councils. It is my hope that even as such paragovernment councils are mobilized, their agents and movements will still participate in the civic forms of standing government, and that representatives and leaders in the standing government will incorporate the fresh insights and voices of conciliar movements. Within the federal government are some real resources for valuable change, and these should not be squandered as citizens move to embrace the options like the movement conciliarism I suggest here. But I harbor significant skepticism today about the extent of the standing government's willingness or ability to respond democratically to the most pressing demands of its people. In all likelihood, given the federal government's corrosion into a regime of imperial design, its addiction to war, its wartime economics, its being beholden to corporate planners and managers accommodating an ever more anti-liberal modernism and exploiting an ever more chauvinistic religious and secular American romanticism—given all this, prophetic spirit's councils will need to prepare for a longer, more protracted struggle, with more dramatic ends in sight.

What this means is that in the post-9/11 USA, prophetic spirit may need to catalyze art, public clamor, and deliberative reasoning, all at work in the democratic councils, in ways that create certain periods of nongovernability for the present leaders of U.S. federal government, or, at least, the serious threat of nongovernability. At their best, those embodying truly revolutionary traditions and expectations in the U.S. have creatively disrupted government business-as-usual, in the name of a greater humanity and more just and peaceful modes of governance. Such disruptions can indeed provoke historic public crises. Some will fear this, as if the majority of U.S. residents and much of the globe have not already been placed in crisis by the regime of power now at work. If we are aware of the disruption already at work, any disruptions and nongovernability provoked by movement conciliarism can be seen as opportunities for the emergence of more democratic forms of governance. This can be done without strategies of violence, as in the 1960s and 1970s through the creative nonviolent actions of diverse civil rights workers and activists like Ella Barker, Martin Luther King Jr., Fannie Lou Hamer, Bob Moses, César Chavez, Dolores Huerta, Yuri Kochiyama, and white activists and supporters from the North and South, all of whom cooperated to provoke significant federal change. Their successes, even though limited in significant ways, were due not only to their own imaginative and sacrificial actions, but also to more militant elements that were on hand in the U.S., for example, supporters of

Malcolm X, the Nation of Islam, the Black Panthers, participants in various Black Power groups, as well as frustrated groups who took to the streets in rioting.[48] Tumult and worries about nongovernability and militants' violence will always be at hand, and they were one part of the situation faced by the nonviolent protestors of the 1960s and 1970s who brought their more powerful commitment to nonviolence onto the scene. Those nonviolent protestors, at their best, creatively engaged the dreams, aspirations, and lives of those with more violent proclivities. Moreover, there also existed a significant international and military pressure from the arrangement of powers in the Cold War period. This helped to force U.S. federal officials to treat their dispossessed peoples in ways that could not be used to their detriment by the Soviet bloc.

There are militant groups in the United States ready to display violence for their ends. They are rarely imbued, however, with the traits of revolutionary belonging and expectation that I have delineated and advocate in this book. If they do share the aims and orientations of prophetic spirit, they should be invited to participate in the councils, and challenged to share in the genres of artistic imagery, public enactment, and deliberative reasoning that are the hallmarks of prophetic spirit. As I noted above, a willingness to engage in these genres functions as a criterion for including dissidents in the category of those manifesting prophetic spirit's revolutionary expectation.

Today there is no Soviet Union partly because of its own legacy of tyranny, oppression, and nondemocratic practice. But radical liberalism will need to construct its councils today so that international leaders, agents, and movements, which are often more mindful than are U.S. officials about the needs of suffering peoples, can exert pressure constructively to change the direction of governance in the United States, not only for U.S. citizens' sakes but for those in nations abroad. In these ways, movement conciliarism in the United States would benefit from the significant leverage that international groups possess.

My advocacy for something like these councils is not new. Often, when marginalized and oppressed groups have faced

overweening powers that concentrated wealth and political decision making in elite echelons of social orders, something like this
conciliarism has had to be practiced. As one example from recent
history, the long repressed and marginalized indigenous Maya
of south Mexico, organizing as the Zapatistas, held their own
national plebiscites throughout Mexico to take votes on key public questions that the Mexican citizenry was not able to vote on in
other ways.[49] This is just one way in which indigenous organizers
sought to create new modes of governmentality amid modernist
structures that often excluded them and many others.[50]

To take an example from the longer witness of history, Cornel
West has recalled the *demes,* or basic political citizens' units, of
ancient Greece. These were organized by peasant groups as a kind
of counter-politics for those who refused to submit to oligarchic
tyrants. They not only revolted but formed these *demes* as centers
of democratic culture. These local forms, emergent in the sixth
century BCE, were crucial enhancements of local democratic processes.[51] Other groups throughout history have sought to craft
such units or councils to create or recreate the power of a people's
commons in the face of abusive power.

West sees the formation of *demes* in Greek history as able to
"instruct and inspire our practice of democratic citizenship in
present-day America."[52] He also sees in this period a spirit of
Socratic questioning, which he deepens and radicalizes with the
prophetic faith traditions and with the tragicomic hope that the
best of the black freedom struggle still brings forward today. With
his characteristic genius and eloquence, West indeed inspires readers to put on the "democratic armor," in his terms, that creatively
weaves Socratic, prophetic, and tragicomic elements. These, be
believes, are the "moral pillars" for safeguarding democratic fervor
and the now fragile "democratic tradition" in North America.[53] As
a further step, I have proposed that prophetic spirit's practices of
revolutionary expectation need to be constituted in the U.S. by a
paragovernmental conciliarism. Something like the *demes,* which
West discusses in passing, needs actually to be called for today.

This need seems especially clear since September 11, 2001, in
the United States. The 9/11 moment has enabled both religious

and secular romanticism and a more virulent contractual liberalism to attain a veritable lockdown on the democratic mechanisms of U.S. government. Elected officials to the U.S. Senate and House of Representatives are dependent for their campaigns on the exorbitant sums that usually only the large corporations can offer. Enacted legislation is more due to the pressure of corporate lobbyists than to legislators listening to their constituencies. The present executive leadership in the regime of George W. Bush has exploited the fear and nationalism spawned by the 9/11 moment to take U.S. peoples into the ignominy and burdens of a disastrous war and occupation in Iraq, and authorized interrogation by torture. The affair in Iraq will serve only those plutocratic few who benefit from the geopolitical control and influence over the flow and pricing of oil and natural gas[54] or from the building and maintenance of U.S. military bases throughout the world.[55]

At the time of this writing, the Bush regime is also calling for the need to radically revise the U.S. Social Security program under the guise of liberating it from a looming future crisis. There does seem to be a crisis ahead in about 2018, when the baby boomer generation hits its strongest retirement years and makes greater demands, causing Social Security to have to draw assets from its trust fund. This problem can be addressed without the major privatization program that the Bush regime touts and also without jeopardizing a program that helps support 47 million of the U.S. population's most needy members.[56] There is a good chance that the challenge Social Security needs to face in the future is not quite the "havoc!" that the Bush regime portrays it to be. Is the Social Security crisis any more real than the announced crisis of weapons of mass destruction that the Bush regime announced as motive for the U.S. invasion of Iraq? Is a government to be believed now about a supposed Social Security crisis when its leaders—Bush, Dick Cheney, and Condoleezza Rice—already have damaged their character and public virtue with hype about Saddam Hussein's weapons of mass destruction, even suggesting that without the U.S. invasion our nation risked a mushroom cloud? By now, this all shouldn't surprise us. As we have seen, the mix of deception and aggressive nationalism seems a near virtue of neoconservative character.

About all this, prophetic spirit indeed mourns and utters its cries of lament and rage. In addition, from its revolutionary tradition and expectation, it presses on to the planning of practices that might forge some counterpower to the imperial specters of American romanticism and contractual liberalism that haunt us today. These specters are here to stay for a very long time unless prophetic spirit grows stronger as their rival specter. Indeed, it can do so, building on the agents and genres of revolutionary expectation like those lifted up in this chapter. But they will also have to find their way to practice something like the paragovernmental conciliarism in the United States that I have here proposed. A new league of *demes*—drawing from the insights of other democratic experiments such as the Iroquois League of Five Nations (Six Nations, subsequently),[57] diverse democracies around the world, and the two-hundred-year-old experiment of the United States—needs to be brought forward now.

Prophetic spirit is a specter to the currents of American romanticism and contractual liberalism that bedevil the nation and world today. Prophetic spirit's agents are alive with aesthetic imagination and resistance, with courage to make public and diverse kinds of clamor on behalf of marginalized and repressed peoples, and with discipline for deliberative reasoning to bring forward new planning and practices. What will become of the current structures and systems of U.S. empire and managerial elitism today may depend on whether government is at all open to the radical liberalism of a prophetic spirit. Even more important, though, is whether people will organize alternatives, whether they will orchestrate their movements in relation to one another in ways that embody the traditions and expectations of prophetic spirit. 9/11 as mythic moment is still open, releasing ever-more powerful waves of American romanticism and elite policies of contractual liberalism into the U.S. body politic and global society. These destructive specters of empire may continue to haunt the North American mainland and the world for a long period to come. Again, though, there is the counter-specter: prophetic spirit. It is a spirit of revolutionary belonging with centuries of tradition behind it as a resource for change today. It is also a spirit of revolutionary expectation that envisions a radically different future. Who of us will keep prophetic spirit alive in this time? Who among us will enable prophetic spirit to reforge belonging and expectation in the post-9/11 USA?

CHRISTIAN FAITH AND COUNTER·IMPERIAL PRACTICE

Religion, Politics, and the Christian Right has not been an explicitly Christian book, the kind that leads with the symbols and beliefs of Christian faith. I have published two other books that are specifically Christian responses to struggles for liberation in United States contexts—regarding not just matters of empire, but also of white racism, gender injustice, heterosexism and homophobia, economic exploitation, and the ways these complexly interact with one another.[1]

This book has been a departure from previous writings, which gave centrality to Christian symbols and beliefs for addressing contemporary cultural and political issues. No doubt, in this work, the signs of my own Christian background persist. I am working, though, out of a sense that prophetic spirit is nurtured by a broader and more diverse human orientation than is manifested in Christian practices in the U.S. today. But I will continue to work in Christian communities to nurture and support their participation in prophetic spirit.

Why relegate a Christian commentary to this brief epilogue? In the post-9/11 United States of America, so many Christian churches have compromised with, or are buried under, American romanticism and contractual liberalism that it is hard to point to Christian communities as active bearers of prophetic spirit. Christians in the U.S. have too insignificant a presence among the agents and aesthetic imagination of prophetic spirit to be visible as valuable forces for nurturing and manifesting revolutionary belonging and expectation amid the powers of the post-9/11 USA.

A big part of that problem lies in groups of "white moderates," those who in the U.S. benefit from systems that significantly entitle them as white citizens. They may disagree overall with the present imperial regime but at the same time think they can lie back and survive, perhaps even benefit from, imperial adventuring by their government, military, and fellow corporate "citizens." Meanwhile, people of color abroad and also in the U.S. military disproportionately bear the sacrifice of life, limb, and freedom. Many other whites who style themselves as progressives or liberals seem also to remain silent. Martin Luther King Jr.'s scathing words from his *Letter from a Birmingham Jail* still apply: "I must confess that over the last few years I have been greatly disappointed with the white moderate. I have almost reached the regrettable conclusion that the Negro's great stumbling block is not the White Citizen's Council-er or the Ku Klux Klanner, but the white moderate who is more devoted to order than to justice, who prefers a negative peace which is the absence of tension to a positive peace which is the presence of justice."[2] Unless white moderates plan an outright embrace of more brutal and imperial ways, it is time—long past time—for them to take up the way of prophetic spirit's revolutionary belonging and expectation, risking a radical liberalism in search of King's "positive peace which is the presence of justice."

While things may be better among churches of color in the United States, among those who rarely identify with the Christian Right and often vote against it, public life in the U.S. still awaits a vigorously displayed and united prophetic leadership from those churches. All of us must challenge ourselves to nurture the kind of prophetic spirit that enlivens a Christian critique and resistance to the politics of racial and sexual contracts, as well as to the politics of U.S. imperial war and full-spectrum dominance over the global economy and other nations. I certainly include myself among many who need to resist better the way the U.S. imperial regime and ethos pulls us into complicity.

I am also well aware of, and treasure my connections with, those exceptional Christian people and communities who *do* embody prophetic spirit today: the Catholic Workers Movement,

Church Folks for a Better America,[3] the Sojourners' community in Washington, DC, so eloquently represented by the writing of Jim Wallis,[4] and many others interspersed through various
churches and movements, especially in many of the churches of
poor and repressed people within and without the United States
today. Some of my Christian colleagues and friends have lamented
that I wrote this, an "anti-Christian" book. I have not. I have only
sought to write my way forward into a notion of prophetic spirit
that should have pride of place in the North American churches
today. In so doing, I have followed prophetic spirit's migration,
often out of churches and into other more courageous and vigi-
lant citizen movements and structures outside the church. Many
of us are laboring to strengthen and to build a "Christian Left," if
one wants to use that term. In the meantime, this book has been
one I have tried to write, first of all, as a human being and citizen,
one who labors in this imperial moment that is reinforced by the
resurgent Constantinian Christianity in the United States.

To remind us all of the prophetic possibilities carried by a
Christian gospel, however, I want to close with a brief statement
of its main lines, highlighting a prophetic interpretation of the
tradition of Jesus for counterimperial struggle. This can best be
done by reflecting first on the notion of "gospel" and then on an
interpretation of the gospel as "reconciliatory emancipation."

GOSPEL

Christians often use the term "gospel" to speak of some "good
news," "glad tidings"—meanings that are roughly equivalent to
the Greek word *euangelion*. But the term also functions as a marker
of what Christians take to be at stake in holding their faith. There
is no one such understanding of "the gospel," but most Christian
communities work out of some inherited and creatively shaped
view of it and thus have a distinctive sense of what the event of
their faith is. Exploring meanings of "the gospel," then, constitutes one way of considering basic options for Christian public
speech and action. In this section, I set forth an understanding

of "gospel" that has often been subordinated to other concerns in Christian history but that, in these times, may be especially important to recall.

When Paul wrote in his epistle to the Romans that he was "not ashamed of the gospel, for it is the power of God unto salvation" (Romans 1:16), or when Mark later etched the first lines of his Gospel, "The beginning of the Gospel of Jesus Christ . . ." (Mark 1:1), the very word used, "gospel," came loaded with political meaning. The term resonated powerfully with the discourse of the political Caesars and military generals of imperial Rome, and thus in the imperial cult.[5] It was their term for the glad tidings that announced and eulogized Roman military victories or celebrations, and sacrifices made on behalf of the emperor. The emperor was uniquely proclaimed "savior," one who brings world peace, the enforced peace of Roman power, the Pax Romana.

For Mark, Paul, and other early Christians, then, to use the word "gospel" was to take a term from realms of political power and announce Jesus as being the center of a new kind of religio-political movement. To build this new entity, this "kingdom," or realm, around the executed figure of Jesus of Nazareth from Galilee was an especially surprising move. Jesus's execution on a cross placed him among the crucified ones, those who were marked as political threats, alternatives to imperial ways. And however much Jesus's life and teaching went beyond what we often call politics today, in the times of Mark and Paul, this gospel was as political as it was religious.[6]

Remember, too, the emphasis on Jesus of Nazareth as being from Galilee. This site is crucial for understanding the nature of the Jesus movement as political. Galilee was not the pastoral landscape taught in many a tranquil U.S. church environment. Galilee was a site of daily suffering and resistance. Galilee was a district where the rural poor had suffered poverty and indebtedness at the crossroads of empires for centuries, as well as the rhythms of their daily living. Historically, Galileans, like those in other political units, could cooperate with imperial and elitist religious centers of power. Especially as the Gospel writers interpreted Jesus, however, his Galilean connections suggested the risk and danger

of a ministry lived on the underside of empire, mandating a faithfulness to the traditions of the prophets that would be severely
tested within the imperial hegemony of Rome and its often brutal
tyranny.[7]

That Galilee was also the place, according to Mark's Gospel, to
which Jesus returned after his resurrection, where the disciples
were told they might later find him and his spirit to be at work
(Mark 16). That is the place the "speaking Galileans" (Acts 2:7)
were from—those gifted translators who bewildered the "devout
men of every nation" when, on the day of Pentecost (the outpour-
ing of the spirit), people throughout the known world were hearing the gospel in their own languages (Acts 2:1-8).

The Christian gospel, then, is born from the underside of
empire. It has its fundamental meaning as a life of faith and action
for communities that dare to take on empire. It has a power, as
the early Christians knew, not simply to challenge worship of
the emperor, for which early Christians have often been drama-
tized, but also to challenge the habits of empire, the very ways it
builds community. That ability to challenge, to live outside the
imperial frame even when it was seemingly ubiquitous and ruthless, is intrinsic to the power of the gospel. The gospel so understood, especially when Jesus is said to have often quoted the great
Hebrew prophets, could be a resource for prophetic spirit. The
gospel could be part of the specter that spells the termination of
empires, whether of Pax Romana or of Pax Americana.

RECONCILIATORY EMANCIPATION

To develop further this crucial political dimension of Christian
experience, I have often portrayed the gospel, or "the event of
Jesus Christ," with the term "reconciliatory emancipation." I have
explored this notion in earlier works,[8] but here let me highlight
the major points. With this phrase, the gospel is first and foremost
one of emancipation, or liberation, in the sense of announcing
and enacting freedom-making movement. To be sure, we know
well how, from the times of fourth-century Constantinian Chris-

tianity to the present day, Christians have served up obstacles to liberation. They have licensed institutionalized repression, implemented inquisitional terror, and reinforced systems of the worst sort with their powers of religion. The Christian Right—today's "Constantinian Christians" as Cornel West has referred to them— is another prime example of empire-reinforcing Christianity.

In addition to the long history of Christians' oppressive actions, even the liberation theologies have been far from perfect. We need to learn from past mistakes, for example, of those twentieth-century liberation theologians who often ignored whole sectors of the very "poor" whom liberation theologians claimed to champion: women, indigenous peoples, and racially oppressed groups.[9] There is nothing new about radical Christian theologies and politics failing to live up to their ideals. It has happened before; it will happen again. That does not mean that we can let go of the focus on liberation and its radical politics. For all of its flaws, for all of the changes that liberation theology has exhibited in recent years, it has the indispensable virtue of mining the power of a gospel of liberation from the preaching and teaching of the global church. This liberation theology can be seen as a present-day manifestation of the "liberation theology" that has been carried throughout the history of the revolutionary Atlantic, working among the "motley crew" described so eloquently by Peter Linebaugh and Marcus Rediker in The Many-Headed Hydra.[10]

By "emancipation" I mean a practical effort and participation in movements of liberation from every kind of oppressive dynamic and also to, or into, structured communities that sustain, criticize, reformulate, and develop practices and theories of liberation. Liberation, in this sense, is especially marked by its capacity and willingness to challenge imperial rule, because that kind of rule entails a comprehensive attempt to subordinate and oppress. The liberating work can take the form of artistic imagery, public demonstration and organizing, as well as intellectual critique.

I also emphasize, however, that the gospel of liberation needs to be qualified by the notion of reconciliation. Without forfeiting the primacy of the liberation motif, Christian experiences of emancipation, at their best, seek also to make and embrace unities, to reconcile differences. The struggle with differences is always an intertwined yet distinctive aspect of the struggle for liberation amid oppression. These differences may be set by the diverse groups struggling for liberation: people who suffer gender injustice or racial injustice, people without a functioning democracy, nature itself groaning for respect and care. Most intensely, perhaps, the reconciliatory qualifier also means that Christian liberatory practice even aims to build some kind of community with perceived enemies. Thus, as in the liberation theology of Peruvian theologian Gustavo Gutiérrez, Christian love is extended even to the adversary of love, to the violators of liberation. Such a love of the enemy can be compatible with both a preferential option for the poorest and a sustained adversarial practice for them.

So the qualifier "reconciliatory" holds the liberating politics of the gospel open to a multiplicity of different sites of awareness and action: aesthetic, psychological, personal/individual, social, mystical/meditative. Christians do many things in their communities that go well beyond their practicing a politics of liberation. Yet the going beyond to these many other realms is a going beyond that best *goes through and not around* the political practice of liberation. I know my claim for the political character of the gospel of reconciliatory liberation *is* a strong one, but it is not reductionist in the sense of overlooking the many other facets and features of Christian experience. It does not reduce the totality of all Christian experience to the practice of liberation.

Christian public witness, then, is the process of Christians living out practices of liberation in a reconciliatory way. Embracing the gospel in this sense would allow Christian communities to participate in—indeed, to generate—the prophetic spirit needed in a post-9/11 context of Pax Americana and U.S. imperial practice. If they led with a commitment to emancipation, with a spirituality that thrived on the full political force of emancipation, Christian communities could find themselves a part of the revolutionary subjectivity and tradition, the motley crew that remains the carrier of revolutionary expectation for the future.

Moreover, an emancipating praxis understood as "reconciliatory," open also to navigating differences, might be crucial for nurturing the diversity and openness to mutual critique that a prophetic conciliarism will need today, especially as it seeks to practice deliberative reasoning. Holding ourselves accountable to others' critique requires being steeped in some degree of self-limiting, as well as self-asserting, discourse for building emancipatory structures. Christians have often used their pleas for love and reconciliation to subvert demands for justice and liberation. This has often permitted the liberalism of a repressive tolerance, one that seems not to take a stand and that has often been a function of many Christian rhetorics of reconciliation. At their best, though, Christian practices of reconciliation might contribute a dimension of "listening love," a liberal discipline so necessary for the deliberative reasoning in prophetic struggle. That kind of love does not lessen the urgency or thoroughgoing concerns of revolutionary justice and emancipation; in fact, it can enhance and strengthen them. That kind of Christian rhetoric of reconciliation as listening love in the struggle for liberation can help yield a more radical liberalism.

In these ways, Christians can still nurture the prophetic spirit that takes on empires. Indeed, they are often doing so throughout the world. In the United States, however, counterimperial Christian groups are few and far between. May they one day grow stronger.

NOTES

PREFACE

1. Tariq Ali, *The Clash of Fundamentalisms: Crusades, Jihads and Modernity* (New York: Verso, 2002).

2. Michael Hout and Andrew M. Greeley, "A Hidden Swing Vote: Evangelicals," *The New York Times,* 4 September 2004, A17.

3. Jim Wallis, *God's Politics: A New Vision for Faith and Politics in America* (San Francisco: HarperSanFrancisco, 2005).

4. For further study of terminology for the groups that make up conservative Protestants, see sociologists Robert D. Woodberry and Christian S. Smith, "Fundamentalism et al.: Conservative Protestants in America," *Annual Review of Sociology* 24 (1998): 25–56.

5. Anatol Lieven, *America Right or Wrong: An Anatomy of American Nationalism* (New York: Oxford University Press, 2004), 7, 20–22, 23, 27–28.

6. Walter LaFeber, *Inevitable Revolutions: The U.S. in Central America,* 2nd ed. (New York: Norton, 1993), 19–39.

INTRODUCTION:
FAITH, AMERICAN EMPIRE, AND SPIRIT

1. *George W. Bush: Faith in the White House,* DVD (New York: Good Times Home Video, 2004).

2. Quoted from "Restoring Scientific Integrity in Policymaking," a statement from the Union for Concerned Scientists, in *With God on Their Side: How Christian Fundamentalists Trampled Science, Policy, and Democracy in George W. Bush's White House,* ed. Esther Kaplan (New York: The New Press, 2004), 95, 291n12. The full statement is available at www.ucsusa.org/global_environment/rsi/page.cfm?pageID=1320.

3. Kaplan, *With God on Their Side*, 34, 35, 96.

4. Ibid., 24, 59–63.

5. Ibid., 20–23.

6. Walter D. Mignolo, *Local Histories/Global Designs: Coloniality, Subaltern Knowledges, and Border Thinking* (Princeton: Princeton University Press, 2000), 251, 281.

7. Emmanuel Todt, *After the Empire: The Breakdown of the American Order* (New York: Columbia University Press, 2002).

8. Andrew D. Bacevich, *American Empire: The Realities and Consequences of U.S. Diplomacy* (Cambridge: Harvard University Press, 2002), 133.

9. Niall Ferguson, *Colossus: The Price of America's Empire* (New York: Penguin Press, 2004), 12–19, 28–29, 298–301.

10. Les Roberts, Riyadh Lafta, Richard Garfield, Jamal Kudhain, and Gilbert Burnham, "Mortality Before and After the 2003 Invasion of Iraq: Cluster Sample Survey," *The Lancet* vol. 364, no. 9448 (November 2004): 1,857–64. For debates on this report, see accompanying "Comments." See also the press release from Iraq Body Count, "Iraq Death Toll Spirals Upwards; Elections Followed by Increase in Civilian Casualties," www.iraqbodycount.net/press (17 March 2005). In remembrance, Iraq body count has compiled a list of names for over three thousand of the Iraqi civilians killed.

11. Chris Hedges, *War Is a Force That Gives Us Meaning* (New York: Public Affairs, 2002), 3, 28, 17.

12. Richard Slotkin, *The Fatal Environment: The Myth of the Frontier in the Age of Industrialization, 1800–1890* (Norman: University of Oklahoma Press, 1985), 33–39.

13. Anatol Lieven, *America Right or Wrong: An Anatomy of American Nationalism* (Princeton: Princeton University Press, 2004), 217.

14. William Julius Wilson, *The Bridge over the Racial Divide: Rising Inequality and Coalition Politics*, Aaron Wildavsky Forum for Public Policy 2 (Berkeley: University of California Press, 1999).

15. Christian Parenti, *The Soft Cage: Surveillance in America from Slavery to the War on Terror* (New York: Verso Books, 2003); Andrew P. Napolitano, *Constitutional Chaos: What Happens When the Government Breaks Its Own Laws* (Nashville: WND Books, 2004).

16. United Nations General Assembly, "Declaration against Torture," December 9, 1975, quoted in Edward Peters, *Torture: Expanded Edition* (Philadelphia: University of Pennsylvania Press, 1996), 273–84.

17. Karen J. Greenberg and Joshua L. Dratel, eds., "Appendix C" in *The Torture Papers: The Road to Abu Ghraib* (New York: Cambridge University Press, 2005), 1,241.

18. "Pentagon Admits Use of Torture Manuals," *National Catholic Reporter*, 4 October 1976.

19. Michael Ratner and Ellen Ray, *Guantánamo: What the World Should Know* (White River Junction, Vt.: Chelsea Green, 2004).

20. Ibid., xvii.

21. In addition to Greenberg and Dratel's *The Torture Papers,* see also Mark Danner, *Torture and Truth: America, Abu Ghraib, and the War on Terror* (New York: New York Review of Books, 2004).

22. Quoted in Jane Meyer, "Outsourcing Torture," *The New Yorker* (14 and 21 February 2005): 112.

23. Ibid.

24. Jacobo Timmerman, *Prisoner without a Name, Cell without a Number,* trans. Tony Talbot (New York: Vintage Books, 1988), 32–33.

25. William T. Cavanaugh, *Torture and Eucharist: Theology, Politics, and the Body of Christ* (Malden, Mass.: Blackwell, 1998), 34.

26. On Ezekiel and other prophets in relation to the Hebrew *nabi,* see H.-P. Muller, *"Nabi,* et al." in *Theological Dictionary of the Old Testament,* vol. 9., ed. G. J. Botterwerk, H. Ringgren, and H.-J. Fabry, trans. David E. Green (Grand Rapids, Mich.: William B. Eerdmans, 1998), 129–50, esp. 147.

27. Jeffrey Stout, *Democracy and Tradition* (Princeton: Princeton University Press, 2003), 173. He is specifically discussing Seyla Benhabib, a Turkish-born U.S. feminist, in this case.

28. Susan Jacoby, *Freethinkers: A History of American Secularism* (New York: Metropolitan Books, 2004), 10–11.

29. I am here adapting an understanding of the "spiritual" from Peter J. Paris, *The Spirituality of African Peoples: The Search for a Common Moral Discourse* (Minneapolis: Fortress Press, 1995), 22. Paris's notion expresses his reflection on African spiritual traditions as well as his work with the religious viewpoints of Paul Tillich.

30. These two currents, American romanticism and contractual liberalism, are roughly analogous to Paul Tillich's "political romanticism" and "bourgeois society," as developed in his 1933 book, *The Socialist Decision,* in which he analyzed the 1930s political scene in Germany (trans. Franklin Sherman [New York: Harper & Row, 1977]).

31. Michael Lind, *The Next American Nation: The New Nationalism and the Fourth American Nation* (New York: The Free Press, 1995), 139–80.

1. Evil in Public Life Today

1. Peter Singer, *The President of Good and Evil: The Ethics of George W. Bush* (New York: Dutton, 2004), 209.

2. Peter Brown, *Augustine of Hippo: A Biography* (Berkeley: University of California Press, 1967), 46–48, 148–50.

3. Jean Bethke Elshtain, *Just War against Terror: The Burden of American Power in a Violent World* (New York: Basic Books, 2003). This book was published in April, approximately one month after the launching of the U.S. invasion of Iraq.

4. Francis Fukuyama, "The Neoconservative Moment," *The National Interest* (Summer 2004), and Ezzat Ibrahim, "Open-Ended History," interview with Francis Fukuyama, *Al-Ahram Online* 688, 29 April–5 May 2004; http://weekly.ahram.org.eg/2004/688/intrvw.htm.

5. Institute for American Values, "Pre-Emption, Iraq, and Just War: A Statement of Principles," 14 November 2002; http://www.americanvalues.org/html/1b___pre-emption.html.

6. See, for example, Paul Berman, "Listening to Terrorists," *New York Times Book Review,* 27 April 2003.

7. This position is evident in the statement "How We Can Coexist," which was signed and released by 153 Saudi scholars on October 23, 2002. It remains posted on the *Islam Today* web site at http://www.islamtoday.net/english/showme2.cfm?cat_id=29&sub_cat_id=471.

8. Elshtain, *Just War against Terror,* 184.

9. David E. Stannard, *American Holocaust: Columbus and the Conquest of the New World* (New York: Oxford University Press, 1992).

10. Daniel Yergin, *The Prize: The Epic Quest for Oil, Money, and Power* (New York: Simon & Schuster, 1991), and Michael T. Klare, *Resource Wars: The New Landscape of Global Conflict* (New York: Metropolitan Books, 2001).

11. Said K. Aburish, *The Rise, Corruption, and Coming Fall of the House of Saud* (New York: St. Martin's Press, 1996).

12. On Haiti, see Paul Farmer, *The Uses of Haiti* (Monroe, Maine: Common Courage Press, 1994). On Nicaragua and Guatemala, see Walter Lafeber, *Inevitable Revolutions: The United States in Central America,* 2nd ed. (New York: W. W. Norton, 1993), 225–42, 255–61, respectively. For the U.S. in Argentina, see Marguerite Feitlowitz, *A Lexicon of Terror: Argentina and the Legacies of Torture* (New York: Oxford University Press, 1998), 8–12.

13. Peter Kornbluh, *The Pinochet File: A Declassified Dossier on Atrocity and Accountability* (New York: New Press, 2004), and Philip Shenon, "U.S. Releases Files on Abuses in Pinochet Era," *The New York Times,* 1 July 1999.

14. Peter Dale Scott, "The United States and the Overthrow of Sukarno, 1965–1967," *Pacific Affairs: An International Review of Asia and the Pacific,* vol. 58, no. 2 (Summer 1985): 239–64.

15. Amy Kaplan, "'Left Alone with America': The Absence of Empire in the Study of American Culture," in *Cultures of United States Imperialism,* ed.

Amy Kaplan and Donald E. Pease (Durham, N.C.: Duke University Press, 1993), 8, 20n7.

16. Nelson Mandela, *Long Walk to Freedom: The Autobiography* (Randburg, South Africa: Macdonald Purnell, 1994), 424.

17. Chalmers Johnson, *The Sorrows of Empire: Militarism, Secrecy, and the End of the Republic* (New York: Metropolitan Books, 2004), 204–7 (on Greece), 203–4 (on Spain).

18. Christopher Simpson, *The Splendid Blonde Beast: Money, Law, and Genocide in the Twentieth Century* (New York: Grove Press, 1993).

19. Samantha Power, *"A Problem from Hell": America and the Age of Genocide* (New York: Basic Books, 2002).

20. Elshtain, *Just War against Terror,* 188.

21. Ibid., 215n17.

22. As just one example of sustained and cogent critiques of U.S. imperialism, see Amy Kaplan, *The Anarchy of Empire in the Making of U.S. Culture* (Cambridge: Harvard University Press, 2002).

23. Elshtain, *Just War against Terror,* 180.

24. Ibid.

25. Mark Juergensmeyer, *Terror in the Mind of God: The Global Rise of Religious Violence* (Berkeley: University of California Press, 2000), 126–33.

26. Bassam Tibi, *The Challenge of Fundamentalism: Political Islam and the New World Disorder* (Berkeley: University of California Press, 2002), 12–15.

27. Elshtain, *Just War against Terror,* 31.

28. Ibid., 5.

29. Ibid., 181.

30. Mark Lewis Taylor, "We Can Trace Roots of Terror to Ourselves," *Newark Star Ledger,* 17 October 2001, 29.

31. Henry Packler, *Weimar Etudes* (New York: Columbia University Press, 1982), 75.

32. Paul Tillich, *Against the Third Reich: Paul Tillich's Wartime Radio Broadcasts to Nazi Germany,* ed. Ronald H. Stone and Matthew Lon Weaver, trans. Matthew Lon Weaver (Louisville: Westminster John Knox Press, 1988), 5.

33. Elshtain, *Just War against Terror,* 103.

34. Ibid., 180.

35. Paul Tillich, "The Intelligentsia and Germany's Conquest," broadcast 4 September 1942, in *Against the Third Reich,* 56.

36. Paul Tillich, "Spiritual Problems of Postwar Reconstruction" (1942), in *The Protestant Era,* trans. James Luther Adams (Chicago: University of Chicago Press, 1948), 261.

37. Paul Tillich, "Storms of Our Times" (1942), in *The Protestant Era,* 238–42.

38. Ibid., 252.

39. "Manichaeism," *The Encyclopedia of Religion*, vol. 10, ed. Mircea Eliade (New York: Macmillan, 1987), 79–94.

40. Elshtain, *Just War against Terror,* 180. Elshtain's treatments of Augustine are more nuanced on these points in two of her books, *Augustine and the Limits of Politics* (Notre Dame, Ind.: University of Notre Dame Press, 1995), and *Who Are We? Critical Reflections and Hopeful Possibilities* (Grand Rapids, Mich.: William B. Eerdmans, 2000). Still, in neither of these books does Elshtain apply her interpretations of Augustine on evil to a critique of the history of European or U.S. imperialism or neocolonialism.

41. On "the sense of the force of past habit in delight," see Peter Brown, *Augustine of Hippo: A Biography* (Berkeley: University of California Press, 1967), 149–50, 154–55.

42. Brown, *Augustine*, 210.

43. St. Augustine, *The City of God* in Philip Schaff, ed., *A Select Library of the Nicene and Post-Nicene Fathers of the Christian Church,* volume 2 (Grand Rapids, Mich.: William B. Eerdmans, 1973), bk. XII, ch. 9, p. 231 (emphasis added).

44. In discussing a Christian theologian and some New Testament notions, I do not propose Christianity and its New Testament as the final word on aspects of evil. My summary is only designed to illustrate an important criticism of Manichaean tendencies that other religious and secular thinkers have also made.

45. Lance Morrow, *Evil: An Investigation* (New York: Basic Books, 2003), 5. In the immediate aftermath of 9/11 Morrow seems to have yielded to the public rhetoric of evil, deploying more Manichaean formulations. See Lance Morrow, "The Case for Rage and Retribution," *Time,* 12 September 2001; http://www.time.com/time/nation/article/0,8599,174641,00.html.

46. Friedrich Schleiermacher, *The Christian Faith,* ed. H. R. Mackintosh and J. S. Stewart (Minneapolis: Fortress Press, 1976 [1830]), section 71, 288.

47. Singer, *The President of Good and Evil,* 207–12.

48. Cited in Singer, *The President of Good and Evil,* 99. Singer is quoting Howard Fineman, "Bush and God," *Newsweek*, 10 March 2003, 22.

49. On these qualities in Bush, see the careful analysis of Ron Suskind, "Faith, Certainty, and the Presidency of George W. Bush," *The New York Times Magazine,* 17 October 2004, 44–51, 64, 102, 106.

50. Paul Tillich, *The Interpretation of History* (New York: Charles Scribner's Sons, 1936), 77–102.

51. Ibid., 93.

52. Edward Epstein, "Success in Afghan War Hard to Gauge," *San Francisco Chronicle,* 23 March 2002; http://www.globalsecurity.org/org/news/2002/020323-attack01.htm.

53. William F. Schulz, "Annual Report: Statement of Dr. William F. Schulz, Executive Director, Amnesty International USA, May 25, 2005." See www.amnestyusa.org/annualreport/statement.html.

2. THE 9/11 MOMENT

1. *Reader's Companion to American History,* ed. Eric Foner and John A. Garraty, s.v. "Trail of Tears" (Boston: Houghton Mifflin, 1991), 1,081.

2. Peter Kornbluh, *The Pinochet File: A Declassified Dossier on Atrocity and Accountability* (New York: The New Press, 2004), and Philip Shenon, "U.S. Releases Files on Abuses in Pinochet Era," *The New York Times,* 1 July 1999.

3. National Commission on Terrorist Attacks Upon the U.S., *The 9/11 Commission Report: Final Report of the National Commission on Terrorist Attacks upon the U.S.* (New York: Barnes & Noble, 2004), 311. As the above comments about Cherokee losses on U.S. soil indicate, this claim needs to be challenged, or at least qualified.

4. See former judge Andrew P. Napolitano, *Constitutional Chaos: What Happens When the Government Breaks Its Own Laws* (Nashville: WND Books, 2004), 92, 146, 180. For monitoring of the U.S. PATRIOT Act, see the website discussion of the Act by the Electronic Frontier Foundation, at http://www.eff.org/patriot. The Electronic Frontier Foundation is an organization seeking to defend civil liberties in areas of technology.

5. Paul Krugman, "A No-Win Outcome," *The New York Times,* 21 December 2001.

6. Shaun Waterman, United Press International, "Whistleblowers Slam 9/11 Report, Reforms," *The Washington Times,* 14 September 2004; http://washingtontimes.com/upi-breaking/20040913-093457-9478r.htm.

7. Benjamin DeMott, "Whitewash as Public Service: How *The 9/11 Commission Report* Defrauds the Nation," *Harper's Magazine* (October 2004): 35–45.

8. On the notion of "American exceptionalism" and in relation to the "myth of the frontier," see Richard Slotkin, *The Fatal Environment: The Myth of the Frontier in the Age of Industrialization, 1800–1890* (Norman: Oklahoma University Press, 1985), 33–47.

9. Frances Fitzgerald, *Way Out There in the Blue: Reagan, Star Wars, and the End of the Cold War* (New York: Simon & Schuster, 2000), 24.

10. G. Simon Harak, "One Nation Under God: The Soteriology of SDI," *Journal of the American Academy of Religion* vol. 56, no. 3 (Fall 1998): 497–527.

11. On theories of myth and the importance of mythic self-understanding in U.S. history see Richard Slotkin, *Gunfighter Nation: The Myth of the Frontier in Twentieth-Century America* (Norman: Oklahoma University Press, 1998), 5–27, 624–60.

12. For an excellent study of how current politics uses citizen fear for repressive purposes, see Corey Robin, *Fear: The History of a Political Idea* (New York: Oxford University Press, 2004).

13. Steve Holland, "Bush Pushes Congress to Renew Anti-Terrorism Law," *Reuters*, June 9, 2005.

14. Michael Parenti, *Superpatriotism* (San Francisco: City Lights Books, 2004).

15. Luntz Research Co. survey of one thousand adults reported in *USA Today*, 3 October 2001, 19–21. Cited in Samuel Huntington, *Who Are We? America's Great Debate* (New York: The Free Press, 2004), 3, 367.

16. Anatol Lieven, *America Right or Wrong: An Anatomy of American Nationalism* (Princeton: Princeton University Press 2004), 5, 223n6.

17. Ibid., 6.

18. See ibid., 19–47.

19. Ibid., 4–10.

3. THE SPECTER OF AMERICAN ROMANTICISM

1. For further discussion of romanticism in European and U.S. contexts, see Bernard M. G. Reardon, "Romanticism," in *The Blackwell Encyclopedia of Modern Christian Thought,* ed. Alister E. McGrath (London: Blackwell, 1993), 573–79. Also, A. O. Lovejoy's early essay "The Discrimination of Romanticisms" is still important (*Essays in the History of Ideas* [Baltimore: Johns Hopkins University Press, 1948]).

2. Reardon, "Romanticism," 573–79.

3. Richard Slotkin, *Gunfighter Nation: The Myth of the Frontier in Twentieth-Century America* (Norman: University of Oklahoma Press, 1998), 654.

4. *Reader's Companion to American History,* ed. Eric Foner and John A. Garraty, s.v. "Manifest Destiny" (Boston: Houghton Mifflin, 1991), 697–98. Compare this with Eldon Kenworthy, *America/Américas: Myth in the Making of U.S. Policy toward Latin America* (University Park: Pennsylvania State University Press, 1995).

5. Thomas Paine, *Common Sense,* in *Collected Writings,* ed. Eric Foner (New York: The Library of America, 1995), 5.

6. Gary Dorrien, *Imperial Designs: Neoconservatism and the New Pax Americana* (New York: Routledge, 2005), 17.

7. In making both of these distinctions in American romanticism— between religious and secular forms, and conservative and revolutionary forms—I am adapting certain elements of Tillich's analysis of German culture in the 1930s. See Paul Tillich, *The Socialist Decision*, trans. Franklin Sherman (New York: Harper & Row, 1977), 27–29.

8. Martin E. Marty, *Righteous Empire: The Protestant Experience in America* (New York: The Dial Press, 1970), 35–45.

9. Rick Perlstein, "The Jesus Landing Pad," *The Village Voice,* 18 May 2004.

10. See Frum's disconcerting experience in David Frum, *The Right Man: The Surprise Presidency of George W. Bush* (New York: Random House, 2003), 3–4.

11. James Mann, *The Rise of the Vulcans: The History of Bush's War Cabinet* (New York: Viking, 2004).

12. Paul Krugman, *The Great Unraveling: Losing Our Way in the New Century* (New York: W. W. Norton, 2004), 8.

13. *George W. Bush: Faith in the White House*, DVD (New York: Good Times Home Video, 2004).

14. *Frontline: The Jesus Factor* (New York: PBS DVD Video, 1999).

15. Kevin Phillips, *American Dynasty: Aristocracy, Fortune, and the Politics of Deceit in the House of Bush* (New York: Viking, 2004), 224.

16. Bush's reference to the Bible as a "guidebook" is in *The Jesus Factor* video. Frum's quote is from Esther Kaplan, *With God on Their Side: How Christian Fundamentalists Trampled Science, Policy, and Democracy in George W. Bush's White House* (New York: The New Press, 2004), 5.

17. Kaplan, *With God on Their Side,* 5.

18. Ibid., 44.

19. Ibid., 81.

20. Ibid.

21. Clifford C. Geertz, "Religion as a Cultural System," in *The Interpretation of Cultures* (New York: Basic Books, 1973), 90. One can find this part of Geertz's theory of religion helpful while also acknowledging the ways his approach to religion has been debated and criticized since the 1970s.

22. Kaplan, *With God on Their Side,* 44–45.

23. Ibid., 72.

24. Ibid., 223.

25. Ibid., 140.

26. Ibid., 134–35.

27. The incident was reported widely in the press. See the CNN report at http://www.cnn.com/2005/POLITICS/04/24/justice.sunday.

28. Ibid., 34.

29. Anatol Lieven, *America Right or Wrong: An Anatomy of American Nationalism* (Princeton: Princeton University Press, 2004), 145, and Nicholas D. Kristof, "Apocalypse (Almost) Now," *The New York Times,* 24 November 2004, A23.

30. Kaplan, *With God on Their Side,* 283n62. For discussions of the power of Christian Zionist organizations in the U.S., see Lieven at pages 23–33.

31. John K. Cooley, *An Alliance against Babylon: The U.S., Israel, and Iraq* (London: Pluto Press, 2005), 4–5, 175–200. Cooley argues that the war plans against Iraq had their first origins even before the catastrophic assaults of September 11, 2001 (see pages 4 and 185, for just the most succinct statements).

32. Ibid., 74.

33. Sarah Posner, Independent Media Institute, "Secret Society," *Alter-Net.com*, 1 March 2005, http://www.alternet.org/story/21372. The conspiracy theory–type title of this essay may be off-putting, but the research is rich and informative.

34. See the statistics at the Pew Research Center for the People and the Press, "Religion and the Presidential Vote," 6 December 2004; online at http://people-press.org/commentary/displayphp3?AnalysisID=103.

35. Michael Hout and Andrew M. Greeley, "A Hidden Swing Vote: Evangelicals," *The New York Times*, 4 September 2004, A17.

36. Kaplan, *With God on Their Side,* 271.

37. Gary Dorrien, *The Neoconservative Mind: Politics, Culture, and the War of Ideology* (Philadelphia: Temple University Press, 1993), and *Imperial Designs: Neoconservatism and the New Pax Americana* (New York: Routledge, 2004), 7.

38. Dorrien, *Imperial Designs,* 78.

39. Ibid., 9; Irving Kristol, *Reflections of a Neoconservative: Looking Back, Looking Ahead* (New York: Basic Books, 1983).

40. Dorrien, *Imperial Designs,* 15.

41. Andrew J. Bacevich, *American Empire: The Realities and Consequences of U.S. Diplomacy* (Cambridge: Harvard University Press, 2002), 133. Exact citation in General John M. Shalikashvili, *Joint Vision 2010* (Washington, DC, 1996), 2.

42. William Safire, "Kerry, Newest Neocon," *The New York Times*, 4 October 2004, A25.

43. Chalmers A. Johnson, *The Sorrows of Empire: Militarism, Secrecy, and the End of the Republic* (New York: Metropolitan Books, 2004), 17.

44. Dorrien, *Imperial Designs,* 17.

45. Ibid., 130.

46. Patrick E. Taylor, "Excerpts from Pentagon's Plan: Prevent the Re-Emergence of a New Rival," *New York Times*, 8 March 1992, A14.

47. Dorrien, *Imperial Designs*, 143.

48. Project for the New American Century, *Rebuilding America's Defenses: Strategies, Forces, and Resources for a New Century* (Washington, DC: Project for a New American Century, 2000), iv.

49. Dorrien, *Imperial Designs,* 3.

50. Ibid.

51. Michael Elliott and James Carney, "First Stop, Iraq," *Time* (31 March 2003): 177, quoted in Ivo H. Daalder and James M. Lindsay, *America Unbound:*

The Bush Revolution in Foreign Policy (Washington, DC: Brookings Institution Press, 2003), 132.

52. See Seymour M. Hersh, *Chain of Command: The Road from 9/11 to Abu Ghraib* (New York: HarperCollins, 2004), and Anonymous [Michael Schener, counterterrorism expert and former CIA member], *Imperial Hubris: Why the West is Losing the War on Terror* (Washington, DC: Brassey's, 2004).

53. Dorrien, *Imperial Designs*, 15–16.

54. Richard Slotkin, *Gunfighter Nation: The Myth of the Frontier in Twentieth-Century America* (Norman: Oklahoma University Press, 1998), 49–56.

55. Thomas Donnelly and Vance Serchuk, "Toward a Global Cavalry: Overseas Rebasing and Defense Transformation," *National Security Outlook, AEI Online,* 1 July 2003; http://www.aei.org/publications/pubID.17783,filter.all/pub_detail.asp.

56. Dorrien, *Imperial Designs*, 15. Just as neocons are by no means all Republicans, they are also *not* all Jewish, unlike what many have inferred from the fact that some prominent neoconservatives are Jewish and cultivate close ties with the Likkud in Israel.

57. Shadia B. Drury, *Leo Strauss and the American Right* (New York: St. Martin's Press, 1997), 148–49.

58. Kaplan, *With God on Their Side,* 177–82. These audits were performed mainly, but not only, against AIDS activists who voiced criticism of U.S. policy relating to the global AIDS epidemic.

59. Bob Woodward, *Bush at War* (New York: Simon & Schuster, 2002), 145–46.

60. Lieven, *America,* 88.

61. Ibid., 91.

62. Michael Lind, *Made in Texas: George W. Bush and the Southern Takeover of American Politics* (New York: Basic Books, 2003).

63. On this dynamic, see Thomas Frank, *What's the Matter with Kansas? How Conservatives Won the Heart of America* (New York: Metropolitan Books, 2004), 102–9.

64. Lieven, *America,* 218.

65. Johnson, *The Sorrows of Empire,* 12–13, 311–12.

4. The Specter of Contractual Liberalism

1. Anatol Lieven, *America Right or Wrong: An Anatomy of American Nationalism* (New York: Oxford University Press, 2004), 49.

2. Fred Siegel, "Liberalism," in Eric Foner and John A. Garraty, *The Reader's Companion to American History* (Boston: Houghton Mifflin, 1991), 653–56. Some of the most enlightening observations, bridging U.S. and East European discussions of liberalism, are in Ira Katznelson, *Liberalism's Crooked Circle: Letters to Adam Michnik* (Princeton: Princeton University Press, 1996).

3. Jeffrey Stout, *Democracy and Tradition* (Princeton: Princeton University Press, 2004), 130.

4. See Stout's helpful critique of social contract theory in ibid., 81–85.

5. Charles W. Mills, *The Racial Contract* (Ithaca: Cornell University Press, 1997), 64–72.

6. Katznelson, *Liberalism's Crooked Circle*, 18.

7. Carole Pateman, *The Sexual Contract* (Stanford, Calif.: Stanford University Press, 1988), 8, quoted in Mills, *The Racial Contract*, 6.

8. Pateman, *The Sexual Contract,* 8.

9. For an excellent treatment of modernity as a colonial world system, see Walter D. Mignolo, *Local Histories/Global Designs: Coloniality, Subaltern Knowledges, and Border Thinking* (Princeton: Princeton University Press, 2000), 3–45, 278–80, 283–87.

10. Julie K. Ward and Tommy Lee Lott, eds., *Philosophers and Race: Critical Essays* (New York: Blackwell, 2002), and Francis Bacon's *Great Instauration* (1620) as described in Peter Linebaugh and Marcus Rediker, *The Many-Headed Hydra: Sailors, Slaves, Commoners, and the Hidden History of the Revolutionary Atlantic* (Boson: Beacon Press, 2000), 37–49.

11. Andro Linklater, *Measuring America: How an Untamed Wilderness Shaped the United States and Fulfilled the Promise of Democracy* (New York: Walker & Co., 2002).

12. David E. Stannard, *American Holocaust: The Conquest of the New World* (New York: Oxford University Press, 1992), 119.

13. On this as a "crisis of liberalism," see Katznelson, *Liberalism's Crooked Circle*, 64–70.

14. Even amid the boom years of the 1990s, this was reported. See Keith Bradisher, "Widest Gap in Incomes? Research Points to the U.S.," *New York Times,* 27 October 1995, D2.

15. Thomas Cosign, "Rich-Poor Gulf Widens: 'Inequality Matters' Conference Puts Nation on Alert," *CBS.MarketWatch.com,* 1 June 2004.

16. William Julius Wilson, *The Bridge over the Racial Divide: Rising Inequality and Coalition Politics*, Aaron Wildavsky Forum for Public Policy 2 (Berkeley: University of California Press, 1999): 23–25.

17. On disparity in the structure of the global economic order, see William K. Tabb, *The Amoral Elephant: Globalization and the Struggle for Social Justice in the Twenty-First Century* (New York: Monthly Review Press, 2001).

18. Karl Marx, *Capital* (1873), vol. 1, part 1, chap. 1, section 4, in *The Marx-Engels Reader,* 2nd ed., ed. Robert C. Tucker (New York: W. W. Norton, 1978), 321.

19. Nancy C. M. Hartsock, *Money, Sex, and Power: Toward a Feminist Historical Materialism* (Baltimore: Johns Hopkins University Press, 1983).

20. In addition to Mills, see Joel Kovel, *White Racism: A Psychohistory* (New York: Columbia University Press, 1970), and Jürgen Oesterhammel, *Colonialism: A Theoretical Overview,* trans. Shelley L. Frisch (Princeton: Markus Wiener, 2002), 108–9.

21. David Greenberg, *The Construction of Homosexuality* (Chicago: University of Chicago Press, 1988), 347–56.

22. For my more extensive criticisms of capitalism from different vantage points (not just of economics or class), see Mark Lewis Taylor, *Remembering Esperanza: A Cultural-Political Theology for North American Praxis* (Maryknoll, N.Y.: Orbis Books, 1990), 76–149.

23. Kevin Phillips, *Wealth and Democracy: A Political History of the American Rich* (New York: Broadway Books, 2002).

24. Tabb, *The Amoral Elephant,* 9–10.

25. David Batstone, *Saving the Corporate Soul—and (Who Knows?) Maybe Your Own* (San Francisco: Jossey-Bass, 2003).

26. Jeffrey D. Sachs, *The End of Poverty: Economic Possibilities for Our Time* (New York: Penguin Press, 2005), 83.

27. For what is included and not included in the project, see the UN Millennium Project, *Investing in Development: A Practical Plan to Achieve the Millennium Development Goals,* Report to the UN Secretary General (London: Earthscan, 2005).

28. Norman Etherington, *Theories of Imperialism: War, Conquest, and Capital* (London: Croom Helm, 1984), 7–24.

29. Detlev J. K. Peukert, *Weimar Republic: The Crisis of Classical Modernity* (New York: Hill and Wang, 1987), 222–30.

30. Kevin Phillips, *American Dynasty: Aristocracy, Fortune, and the Politics of Deceit in the House of Bush* (New York: Viking, 2004).

31. See the video of George W. Bush speaking as President to corporate funders, in *Fahrenheit 911,* a DVD produced by Michael Moore (New York: Columbia Tristar Home, 2005).

32. Thomas B. Desalt and Jonathan Weisman, "Wall Street Firms Funnel Millions to Bush," *The Washington Post,* 24 May 2004, A04.

33. Carl Boggs, *Imperial Delusions: American Militarism and Endless War* (Lanham, Md.: Rowman & Littlefield, 2005), 23–33.

34. Franz J. Hinkelammert, *Sacrificios humanos y sociedad occidental: Lucifer y la bestia* (San José, Costa Rica: DEI, 1991), 43–49.

35. On modernity's structural capacities for enabling racism and genocidal extermination, see Zygmunt Bauman, *Modernity and the Holocaust*, reprint edition with a new afterward by the author (Ithaca: Cornell University Press, 2001).

36. Shadia B. Drury, *The Political Ideas of Leo Strauss* (New York: St. Martin's Press, 1988), xi.

37. Richard Lacayo, "But Who Has the Power?" *Time* (17 June 1996): 43.

38. Gordon S. Wood, "The Fundamentalists and the Constitution," *The New York Review of Books* vol. 35, no. 2 (18 February 1988); http://www.nybooks.com/articles/4534.

39. Kenneth L. Deutsch and John A. Murley, eds. *Leo Strauss, the Straussians, and the American Regime* (Lanham, Md.: Rowman & Littlefield, 1999).

40. Leo Strauss, *The Rebirth of Classical Political Rationalism: An Introduction to the Thought of Leo Strauss,* selected and introduced by Thomas L. Pangle (Chicago: University of Chicago Press, 1989).

41. Harry V. Jaffa, "Strauss at One Hundred," in *Leo Strauss, the Straussians,* 47–48.

42. Kenneth L. Deutsch, "Leo Strauss, the Straussians, and American Regime," in *Leo Strauss, the Straussians, and the American Regime,* ed. Kenneth L. Deutsch and John A. Murley (Lanham, Md.: Rowman & Littlefield, 1999), 51, 57–58.

43. Leo Strauss, "What Is Liberal Education?" (address, 10th Annual Graduation Exercises of the Basic Program of Liberal Education for Adults, University of Chicago, 6 June 1959). The text is available at http://www.ditext.com/strauss/liberal.html.

44. Shadia B. Drury, *Leo Strauss and the American Right* (New York: St. Martin's Press, 1997), 16.

45. Also, see Elizabeth Drew, "The Neocons in Power," *The New York Review of Books* vol. 50, no. 10 (12 June 2003); http://www.nybooks.com/articles/article-preview?article_id=16378.

46. George W. Bush, "Iraq Is Fully Capable of Living in Freedom" (speech, American Enterprise Institute for Public Policy Research (AEI), Washington DC, 26 February 2003), in *The Iraq War Reader: History, Documents, Opinions,* ed. Micah L. Sifry and Christopher Cerf (New York: Harper Touchstone, 2003), 557–59. In this speech, coming less than a month before the war campaign began against Iraq, Bush laid out his vision for the future of Iraq. Many newspapers, including *The New York Times* (27 February 2003, A1) showed AEI head, William Kristol, hosting and applauding Bush in the background.

47. Joshua L. Dratel, "The Legal Narrative," in *The Torture Papers: The Road to Abu Ghraib,* ed. Karen J. Greenberg and Joshua L. Dratel (New York: Cambridge University Press, 2005), xxi. For a list of approved "aggressive counter-resistance techniques" of torture, see Greenberg and Dratel, *The Torture Papers,* 342–43.

48. Drury, *Leo Strauss and the American Right,* 18.

49. The one clear case of this that Drury puts forth is very obliquely put. See Drury, *The Political Ideas of Leo Strauss,* 6–7.

50. Ibid., 58.

51. Robert Locke, "Leo Strauss: Conservative Mastermind," *FrontPageMagazine.com,* 31 May 2002, http://www.frontpagemag.com/Articles/ReadArticle.asp?ID=1233.

52. Drury, *Leo Strauss and the American Right,* 2. Robert Locke says that Strauss and his followers were "cultish" but only "to an extent, though not in my experience offensively so" in his essay, "Leo Strauss."

53. Leo Strauss, *Persecution and the Art of Writing* (Chicago: University of Chicago Press, 1952), 35–36, quoted in Shadia B. Drury, *Leo Strauss and the American Right* (New York: St. Martin's Press, 1997), 61. See also Drury, *The Political Ideas of Leo Strauss,* chap. 2.

54. Seymour M. Hersh, "Selective Intelligence: Donald Rumsfeld Has His Own Special Sources. Are They Reliable?" *The New Yorker,* 6 May 2003.

55. David Corn, "CIA Report Refutes Bush's Rhetoric," *The Nation,* 9 October 2002.

56. Abram Shulsky and Gary Schmitt, "Leo Strauss and the World of Intelligence (By Which We Do Not Mean Nous)," in *Leo Strauss, the Straussians,* 407–12.

57. Gary Schmitt with Donald Kagan and Thomas Donnelly, *Rebuilding America's Defenses: Strategy, Forces, and Resources for a New Century* (Washington, DC: Project for the New American Century, 2000), 17 (available at www.newamericancentury.org).

58. Seymour M. Hersh, *Chain of Command: The Road from 9/11 to Abu Ghraib* (New York: HarperCollins, 2004), 207.

59. See Wolfowitz's attempts to explain his views about the reasons for citing WMDs in Iraq as motive for U.S. war against Iraq in an interview with *Washington Post* reporter Karen De Young, as transcribed by the U.S. Department of Defense; stored at http://www.defenselink.mil/transcripts/2003/tr20030528-depsecdef0222.html.

60. Paul Wolfowitz (Deputy Secretary of Defense), "Q&A Following IISS Asia Security Conference," *U.S. Department of Defense News Transcript,* 31 May 2003, 5; http://www.defenselink.mil/transcripts/2003/tr20030531-depsecdef0246.html.

61. Alain Frachon and Daniel Vernet, "The Strategist and the Philosopher: Leo Strauss and Albert Wohlstetter," *Le Monde,* 16 April 2003, trans. Normal Madarasz, in *CounterPunch* (2 June 2003): 6; http://www.counterpunch.org/frachon06022003.html.

62. Leo Strauss, *On Tyranny*, revised and enlarged (Ithaca, N.Y.: Cornell University Press, 1963), 93–94.

63. Ibid., 93.

64. Ibid., 94, 207.

65. Irving Kristol, "The Neoconservative Persuasion: What It Is and What It Is Not," *The Weekly Standard* vol. 8, no. 47 (25 August 2003).

66. Drury, *Leo Strauss and the American Right,* 152–53.

67. Michael Lind, *Made in Texas: George W. Bush and the Southern Takeover of American Politics* (New York: Basic Books, 2003), 165.

68. Ibid., 167.

69. Ibid.

5. THE SPECTER OF PROPHETIC SPIRIT

1. Cornel West, *Democracy Matters: Winning the Fight against Imperialism* (New York: Penguin Press, 2004), 114–15.

2. On the "whence" and the "whither" as two ontological roots of political thought, see Paul Tillich, *The Socialist Decision,* trans. Franklin Sherman (New York: Harper & Row, 1977),1–10.

3. Ibid., 18–23, 47.

4. bell hooks, *Feminist Theory: From Margin to Center* (Boston: South End Press, 1984), 103–4.

5. Chalmers A. Johnson, *The Sorrows of Empire: Militarism, Secrecy, and the End of the Republic* (New York: Metropolitan Books, 2004), 110 and 330n12.

6. Janice E. Perlman, *The Myth of Marginality: Urban Poverty and Politics in Rio de Janeiro* (Berkeley: University of California Press, 1976).

7. On my notion of "authentic solidarity" between entitled advocates of the oppressed, on the one hand, and movements led by the oppressed, on the other, see Mark Lewis Taylor, "Subalternity and Advocacy as Kairos for Theology," in *Opting for the Margins: Postmodernity and Liberation in Theology,* ed. Joerg Rieger (New York: Oxford University Press, 2003), 1–28.

8. Bruce C. Birch, *Let Justice Roll Down: The Old Testament, Ethics, and Christian Life* (Louisville: Westminster John Knox, 1991), 121–23, 180–82.

9. Peter Linebaugh and Marcus Rediker, *The Many-Headed Hydra: Sailors, Slaves, Commoners, and the Hidden History of the Revolutionary Atlantic* (Boston: Beacon Press), 93.

10. Marilyn Waring, "The System of National Accounts, or the Measure and Mis-measure of Value and Production in Economic Theory," in *Women's Voices on the Pacific: The International Pacific Policy Congress,* ed. Lenora Foerstel (Washington, DC: Maisonneuve Press, 1991), 63–86.

11. For these categories in an expanded notion of a proletariat, see Linebaugh and Rediker, *The Many-Headed Hydra*, 332–33.

12. Leslie Eaton, "In Din of Bronx, Voices for Peace," *New York Times*, 4 March 2003, B1, B6.

13. On this movement, see www.notinourname.net/index.html.

14. Patrick Tyler, "A New Power in the Streets," *New York Times*, 17 February 2003, A1.

15. DeWayne Wickham, "Of Patriotism and the Public Purse," *The Tennessean*, 28 February 2003, 15A.

16. Julie Salamon, "Mobilizing a Theater of Protest. Again," *New York Times*, 6 February 2003, E1, E5.

17. See especially the listings and links at "Church Folks for a Better America," www.cfba.info. Also, "Why Jews Should Oppose the War," *The New York Times*, full-page advertisement, 21 March 2003, A15, and Laura Pelner, "Princeton Theologians Condemn War," *The Trentonian*, 2 April 2003, 8.

18. Paul Tillich, *Systematic Theology*, vol. 3 (Chicago: University of Chicago Press, 1963), 324.

19. On this notion of spirit as dialectically animating while being "complementary" to matter, not differentiated into a "supernatural" realm as many Western religious systems teach, see anthropologist Barbara Tedlock, *Time and the Highland Maya*, rev. ed. (Albuquerque: University of New Mexico Press, 1992), 42–44. See also philosopher David Abram, *In the Spell of the Sensuous: Perception and Language in a More-Than-Human World* (New York: Pantheon Books, 1996), 237–39.

20. Tillich, *Systematic Theology*, 3:324 (emphasis added).

21. Norman Etherington, *Theories of Imperialism: War, Conquest, and Capital* (London: Croom Helm, 1984), 283.

22. Mark Lewis Taylor, "Tracking Spirit: Theology as Cultural Critique," in *Changing Conversations: Religious Reflection and Cultural Analysis*, ed. Dwight N. Hopkins and Sheila Greeve Davaney (New York: Routledge, 1996), 123–44.

6. REVOLUTIONARY BELONGING

1. For more examples of the founders' contradictions and counterrevolutionary compromises, see Peter Linebaugh and Marcus Rediker, *The Many-Headed Hydra: Sailors, Slaves, Commoners, and the Hidden History of the Revolutionary Atlantic* (Boston: Beacon Press, 2000), 236–40.

2. Ibid., 213–14.

3. Ibid., 216–17.

4. On Native Americans' losses and struggle, see David E. Stannard, *American Holocaust: Columbus and the Conquest of the New World* (New York: Oxford University Press, 1992).

5. Antonio Benítez-Rojo, *The Repeating Island: The Caribbean and the Postmodern Perspective* (Durham, N.C.: Duke University Press, 1997) 71, 199–201.

6. Walter D. Mignolo, *Local Histories/Global Designs: Coloniality, Subaltern Knowledges, and Border Thinking* (Princeton, N.J.: Princeton University Press, 2000), 3–45.

7. Marcus Rediker, *Villains of All Nations: Atlantic Pirates in the Golden Age* (Boston: Beacon Press, 2004).

8. Linebaugh and Rediker, *The Many-Headed Hydra,* 213–14.

9. Ibid., 233.

10. Ibid., 328.

11. For a complete discussion, see ibid., 193–96.

12. Ibid., 174.

13. Ibid., 143–73.

14. For more on this period see E. Lipson, *The Growth of English Society: A Short Economic History* (New York: Henry Holt, 1949), 127–39; Oliver O'Donovan, *The Desire of the Nations: Rediscovering the Roots of Political Theology* (Cambridge: Cambridge University Press, 1996); as well as Linebaugh and Rediker, *The Many-Headed Hydra,* 36–70.

15. Linebaugh and Rediker, *The Many-Headed Hydra,* 26.

16. William Dean, *The Religious Critic in American Culture* (Albany: State University of New York Press, 1994), 177.

17. See Mark Lewis Taylor, *The Executed God: The Way of the Cross in Lockdown America* (Minneapolis: Fortress Press, 2001), 70–154. On the origins of emancipatory religious language, see Oliver O'Donovan, *The Desire of the Nations: Rediscovering the Roots of Political Theology* (Cambridge: Cambridge University Press, 1996).

18. On these ideas, see Dean, *Religious Critic in American Culture,* 82–87, 222–24.

19. Linebaugh and Rediker, *The Many-Headed Hydra,* 3.

20. Ibid., 39.

21. Ibid., 68.

22. Ibid., 234.

23. Ibid., 6.

24. Michael Hardt and Antonio Negri, *Multitude: War and Democracy in the Age of Empire* (New York: Penguin Press, 2004), 214.

7. REVOLUTIONARY EXPECTATION

1. Paul Tillich, *The Interpretation of History,* trans. N. A. Rasetzky (New York: Charles Scribner's Sons, 1936), 85.

2. Ira Katznelson, *Liberalism's Crooked Circle: Letters to Adam Michnik* (Princeton: Princeton University Press, 1996), 17, 26, and 10, respectively.

3. Amy Gutman, *Liberal Equality* (Cambridge: Cambridge University Press, 1980), cited in William Kymlicka, *Contemporary Political Philosophy: An Introduction* (New York: Oxford University Press, 2002), 96.

4. Charles W. Mills, *The Racial Contract* (Ithaca: Cornell University Press, 1997), 137n9.

5. Ann Coulter, *How to Talk to a Liberal (If You Must): The World According to Ann Coulter* (New York: Crown Forum, 2004). Coulter's book is just one representative of this contemporary conservative discourse in the media-driven pop culture of the early-twenty-first-century USA.

6. One of Hauerwas's more famous formulations was "if the gospel is true, the politics of liberalism must be false." For the fuller argument, see Stanley Hauerwas, *A Better Hope: Resources for a Church Confronting Capitalism, Democracy, and Postmodernity* (Grand Rapids, Mich.: Brazos Press, 2000), 124. See Jeffrey Stout's fine discussion of Hauerwas on this point, in *Democracy and Tradition* (Princeton: Princeton University Press, 2004), 140–61.

7. John Milbank, *Theology and Social Theory: Beyond Secular Reason* (Oxford: Blackwell, 1990), 4.

8. Thomas Frank, *What's the Matter With Kansas: How Conservatives Won the Heart of America* (New York: Metropolitan Books, 2004), 113–37; see also Anatol Lieven, on humiliation in "the embittered heartland," in *America Right or Wrong: An Anatomy of American Nationalism* (New York: Oxford University Press, 2004), 88–122.

9. See the website for this group and accompanying links at www.IVAW. net.

10. Stephen Donziger, *The Real War on Crime: Report of the National Criminal Justice Commission* (San Francisco: HarperCollins, 1996), 31.

11. Christian Parenti, *Lockdown America: Police and Prisons in the Age of Crisis* (New York: Verso, 1999), xii.

12. Joy James, ed., *Imprisoned Intellectuals: America's Political Prisoners Write on Life, Liberation, and Rebellion* (Boston: Rowman & Littlefield, 2003), and Assata Shakur et al., *Sparks Fly: Women Political Prisoners and Prisoners of War in the U.S.* (Oakland, Calif.: Regent Press, 1998).

13. One of the best examples of organizing by those without *and* within U.S. prisons can be viewed at www.prisonactivist.org.

14. Robin D. G. Kelley, *Freedom Dreams: The Black Radical Imagination* (Boston: Beacon Press, 2002), 115.

15. Ibid., 116.

16. Robin Wagner-Pacifici, *Discourse and Destruction: The City of Philadelphia versus MOVE* (Chicago: University of Chicago Press, 1994).

17. For the KWRU website, see www.kwru.org.

18. For the CHRI website, see www.itapnet.org/chri, and for NNIRR, see www.nnirr.org.

19. Gloria Anzaldúa, *Borderlands/La frontera: The New Mestiza* (San Francisco: Spinsters/Aunt Lute, 1987), 21.

20. Walter D. Mignolo, *Local Histories/Global Designs: Coloniality, Subaltern Knowledges and Border Thinking* (Princeton: Princeton University Press, 2000), 49–88.

21. Ronald Wright, *Stolen Continents: The Americas through Indian Eyes since 1492* (New York: Houghton Mifflin, 1992), 222.

22. On the historical and present power of this version of the "myth of America," see Eldon Kenworthy, *America/Américas: Myth in the Making of U.S. Policy toward Latin America* (University Park: Pennsylvania State University Press, 1995).

23. Glenn T. Morris, "International Law and Politics: Toward a Right to Self-Determination for Indigenous Peoples," in *The State of Native America: Genocide, Colonization, and Resistance,* ed. M. Annette Jaimes (Boston: South End Press, 1992), 55–86.

24. Ward Churchill, *Struggle for the Land: Indigenous Resistance to Genocide, Ecocide, and Expropriation in Contemporary North America* (Monroe, Maine: Common Courage Press, 1993), 411–15.

25. Ward Churchill, "The Earth Is Our Mother: Struggles for American Indian Land and Liberation in the Contemporary United States," in *The State of Native America,* 139–88.

26. Mark Wallace, *Finding God in the Singing River: Christianity, Spirit, Nature* (Minneapolis: Fortress Press, 2005), 1–25.

27. For one introduction to these movements that receive relatively little mainstream press, see Gini Graham Scott, *Erotic Power: An Exploration of Dominance and Submission* (Toronto: Carol Publishing Group, 1998).

28. Michael Harrington, *Socialism* (New York: E. P. Dutton, 1972). See also Bob Avakian, *Revolution: Why It's Necessary, Why It's Possible, What It's All About,* 4 DVDs (New York: Three Q Productions, 2004).

29. For examples of theory and organizing projects, see www.wsws.org.

30. Michael Hardt and Antonio Negri, *Multitude: War and Democracy in the Age of Empire* (New York: Penguin Press, 2004), 281–91.

31. Charles Marsh, *The Beloved Community: How Faith Shapes Social Justice, from the Civil Rights Movement to Today* (New York: Basic Books, 2005), 88–90.

32. Bakari Kitwana, *The Hip Hop Generation: Young Blacks and the Crisis in African American Culture* (New York: Basic Civitas Books, 2002), 145–74.

33. Andrew Boyd, "Extreme Costume Ball: A New Protest Movement Hits the Streets in Style," *The Village Voice,* 25 July 2000, 46–47.

34. See, for example, United Students Against Sweatshops, at www.studentsagainstsweatshops.org/.

35. Margaret E. Keck and Kathryn Sikkink, *Activists Beyond Borders: Advocacy Networks in International Politics* (Ithaca: Cornell University Press, 1998).

36. Alex Callinicos, *The New Mandarins of American Power: The Bush Administrations Plans for the World* (Cambridge: Polity, 2003), 110–18.

37. Kelley, *Freedom Dreams,* 158.

38. Angela Y. Davis, *Blues Legacies and Black Feminism: Gertrude "Ma" Rainey Harper, Bessie Smith, and Billie Holiday* (New York: Pantheon Books, 1998), 127–29, 164, 180, 183.

39. Ralph Ellison, "Richard Wright's Blues," in *Collected Essays of Ralph Ellison,* ed. John F. Callahan (New York: Modern Library, 1995), 129.

40. Kwame Dawes, *Bob Marley: Lyrical Genius* (London: Sanctuary, 2002), 194.

41. On the value and limitations of the Emerson/Whitman/Guthrie/Dylan/Springsteen tradition in lyric poetry and U.S. popular music, see Bryan K. Garman, *A Race of Singers: Whitman's Working Class Hero from Guthrie to Springsteen* (Chapel Hill: University of North Carolina Press, 2000). See also Robin Denselow, *When the Music's Over: The Story of Political Pop* (Boston: Faber and Faber, 1990).

42. Ray Raphael, *The First American Revolution: Before Lexington and Concord* (New York: The New Press, 2002), 59–67.

43. Leslie Gill, *The School of the Americas: Military Training and Violence in the Americas* (Durham, N.C.: Duke University Press, 2004).

44. Raphael, *The First American Revolution,* 24–25, 41–42, 65–68, 82–84, 95–103.

45. Ibid., 2.

46. Stout, *Democracy and Tradition,* 303–4.

47. Taylor Branch, *Parting the Waters: America in the King Years, 1954–63* (New York: Simon & Schuster, 1988), 138, 140, 713.

48. Howard Zinn, *A People's History of the United States, 1492 to the Present,* Twentieth Anniversary ed. (San Francisco: Harper Collins, 1999), 459–61.

49. John Womack Jr., *Rebellion in Chiapas: An Historical Reader* (New York: The New Press, 1999).

50. On Zapatista struggle amid Mexico's modes of "governmentality," see Nicholas P. Higgins, *Understanding the Chiapas Rebellion: Modernist Visions and the Invisible Indian* (Austin: University of Texas Press, 2004), especially 153–90.

51. Cornel West, *Democracy Matters: Winning the Fight against Imperialism* (New York: Penguin, 2004), 205–6.

52. Ibid., 204.

53. Ibid. 216-8.

54. The best arguments for this are given by Hampton College's Peace and World Security Professor Michael T. Klare in his two books *Resource Wars: The New Landscape of Global Conflict* (New York: Metropolitan Books, 2001) and *Blood and Oil: The Dangers and Consequences of America's Growing Dependency on Imported Petroleum* (New York: Metropolitan Books, 2004).

55. Andrew J. Bacevich, *The New American Militarism: How Americans are Seduced by War* (New York: Oxford University Press, 2005), 229n20.

56. There is a quite even-handed discussion of the debate over Social Security by Roger Lowenstein, "A Question of Numbers," *The New York Times Magazine*, 16 January 2005, 42–47, 72, 76, 78.

57. Alvin M. Josephy Jr., *The Patriot Chiefs: A Chronicle of American Indian Leadership* (New York: Viking, 1961), 28–29.

EPILOGUE:
CHRISTIAN FAITH AND
COUNTERIMPERIAL PRACTICE

1. *Remembering Esperanza: A Cultural-Political Theology for North-American Praxis* (Maryknoll, N.Y.: Orbis, 1990) and *The Executed God: The Way of the Cross in Lockdown America* (Minneapolis: Fortress Press, 2001).

2. Martin Luther King Jr., "Letter from a Birmingham Jail," *The Essential Writings and Speeches of Martin Luther King, Jr.*, ed. James M. Washington (San Francisco: HarperCollins, 1986), 295.

3. See its website, www.cfba.info.

4. Jim Wallis, *God's Politics: Why the Right Gets It Wrong and the Left Doesn't Get It* (San Francisco: HarperSanFrancisco, 2005).

5. Gerhard Kittle, *The Theological Dictionary of the New Testament*, vol. 2, s.v. "Euangelion," trans. Geoffrey W. Bromiley (Grand Rapids, Mich.: William B. Eerdmans, 1964), 707–37, esp. 724–25.

6. For additional bibliography on religious and political dimensions of Christian belief, see sources in Taylor, *The Executed God*, 70–98, 176–82.

7. Sean Freyne, *Jesus: A Jewish Galilean* (New York: T & T Clark, 2004).

8. Taylor, *Remembering Esperanza*, esp. chap. 5.

9. For a self-critique of liberation theology on these points, see the introduction by Gutiérrez to the fifteenth anniversary edition of Gustavo Gutiérrez, *A Theology of Liberation: History, Politics, and Salvation* (Maryknoll, N.Y.: Orbis, 1988), xvii–xxxii.

10. Peter Linebaugh and Marcus Rediker, *The Many-Headed Hydra: Sailors, Slaves, Commoners, and the Hidden History of the Revolutionary Atlantic* (Boston: Beacon Press, 2000).

EPIGRAPH CITATIONS BY CHAPTER

Chapter 1: David Frum and Richard Perle, *An End to Evil: How to Win the War on Terror* (New York: Random House, 2003), 9.

Chapter 2: Walden Bello, *Dilemmas of Domination: The Unmaking of American Empire* (New York: Metropolitan Books, 2005), 2.

Chapter 3: Richard Slotkin, *Gunfighter Nation: The Myth of the Frontier in Twentieth-Century America* (Norman: Oklahoma University Press, 1998), 654.

Chapter 4: Charles W. Mills, *The Racial Contract* (Ithaca: Cornell University Press, 1997), 94.

Chapter 5: Michael Hardt and Antonio Negri, *Empire* (Cambridge: Harvard University Press, 2000), 65.

Chapter 6: Gouverneur Morris, quoted in Ray Raphael, *A People's History of the American Revolution: How Common People Shaped the Fight for Independence* (New York: The New Press, 2001), 24, italics mine.

Chapter 7: Ira Katznelson, *Liberalism's Crooked Circle: Letters to Adam Michnik* (Princeton: Princeton University Press, 1996), 10.

INDEX

abolitionists, 113
abortion, 56, 138
Abu Ghraib, 8, 145, 177n47
Abu-Jamal, Mumia, xiii, 132
Abya Yala, 136
Acts of the Apostles, 160
Adams, Abigail, 146
Adams, John, 121
Adams, Samuel, 12, 113, 116
aesthetics, 119, 120, 141–45, 147,
   149, 154
Afghanistan, 22, 24, 65, 66, 104, 139
Africa, 75, 76, 111, 114, 117, 119, 134
African Americans, 20, 44, 94, 99,
   113, 132–33
Afro-Christianity, 119, 120
Akan, 119
Albright, Madeleine, 64
Ali, Tariq, ix
Allende, Salvador, 21
Al-Qaeda, ix, 23, 32, 33, 65, 90
America/Américas, xii–xiii, 118,
   135–36
American century, 27, 41, 63–4
American Creed, 71–2
American Enterprise Institute (AEI),
   17, 52, 65, 88
American exceptionalism, 39–42, 50,
   52, 54, 63, 66, 70, 123, 170n8;
   and "Frontier Myth," 67
American romanticism. *See* Romanti-
   cism
Amnesty International USA, 169n53
Anabaptists, 121
Anti-liberal modernism, 15, 83–95;
   and neoconservatives, 84–86,
   87–88; as aversion to liberalism,
   86–88 ; as aggressive nationalism, 92–95; as deception, 89–92;
   defined, 84
Anzaldúa, Gloria, 135

Apostolic Congress, 1
Arab nations, 20, 134
Argentina, 21
art, 119–20, 141–42, 144, 150
Ashcroft, John, 1, 55, 59
Asia, 75, 111, 114, 117, 120, 134
Asian Americans, 44, 114, 120, 133,
   143
Asian Dub Foundation, 143
Atlantic context, 12, 111, 114, 116,
   117, 126, 136, 144, 145, 161
Augustine of Hippo, 28–9, 31,
   169n40

Babylon, 119
Bacon, Francis, 76, 121
Barker, Ella, 150
Bauer, Gary, 54
Bello, Walden, 35, 36
belonging being, 15, 16, 48–49, 53,
   70, 72–73, 98, 108, 120, 122
Bennett, William, 88
Bin Laden, Osama, 23
biology, 106
Black, Cofer, 8
Black Panthers, 151
Black Power, 151
blues, 142, 143
Bonhoeffer, Dietrich, 100
borders, 135
Boston, 145
Boston massacre, 115
Boston Tea Party, 115
Boykin, William, 2
Bradley Foundation, 65
Bragg, Billy, 143
Brazil, 78
breath, 105–6
Bright Eyes, 143
Britain, 2, 93, 99, 113, 115, 122. 144
Brown, John, 49

187